ADVANCE PRAISE FOR THE BOOK

'The BJP's unlikely conquest of the North-east was powered by the brilliant commitment of its younger workers, notably Rajat Sethi and Shubhrastha. This book isn't just a fine account of how this success was achieved, it is also a vital insight into the BJP's view of the North-east, so distinct from the conventional, established one so far.'

Shekhar Gupta, chairman and editor-in-chief, ThePrint

'This book will provide an insiders' view of an election that the authors helped swing. In that sense, this participant observation of one of the characters and themes and planning behind the Assam elections will be any political junkie's must-read.'

Arnab Goswami, founder and editor-in-chief, Republic TV

'This book is a significant attempt at understanding the historic assembly polls in Assam in 2016 in the context of the state's contemporary politics and its recent tumultuous history. A good job by two political entrepreneurs.'

Rajeev Bhattacharyya, senior journalist, and author, *Rendezvous with Rebels: Journey to Meet India's Most Wanted Men*

'A fine blend of history, electoral politics and the complex, unfolding narrative of India's North-east.'

Minhaz Merchant, biographer of Rajiv Gandhi and Aditya Birla

'I had invested emotionally in the Assam campaign. This book is a lucid recall of the highs and lows of that journey. It flows like a river, taking the readers through the rich history of the North-east, meandering through the maze of complex regional dynamics, finally ebbing into the sea of an existential crisis caused by illegal migration in the region. A must-read for those interested in the subtle art of politics.'

Himanta Biswa Sarma, cabinet minister, Assam government, and convener, North-East Democratic Alliance

THE LAST BATTLE OF SARAIGHAT

THE LAST BATTLE OF
SARAIGHAT

The Story of the BJP's Rise
in the North-east

Foreword by Ram Madhav

RAJAT SETHI AND
SHUBHRASTHA

PENGUIN
VIKING

An imprint of Penguin Random House

VIKING

USA | Canada | UK | Ireland | Australia
New Zealand | India | South Africa | China | Singapore

Viking is part of the Penguin Random House group of companies
whose addresses can be found at global.penguinrandomhouse.com

Published by Penguin Random House India Pvt. Ltd
4th Floor, Capital Tower 1, MG Road,
Gurugram 122 002, Haryana, India

Penguin
Random House
India

First published in Viking by Penguin Random House India 2017

Copyright © Rajat Sethi and Shubhrastha 2017
Foreword copyright © Ram Madhav 2017

ISBN 9780670090273

Typeset in Adobe Garamond Pro by Manipal Digital Systems, Manipal
Printed at Replika Press Pvt. Ltd, India

www.penguin.co.in

MIX
Paper from
responsible sources
FSC® C016779

This is a legitimate digitally printed version of the book and therefore might not
have certain extra finishing on the cover.

CONTENTS

~

LIST OF ABBREVIATIONS

~

AASU	All Assam Students' Union
ACMS	Assam Chah Mazdoor Sangh
AGP	Asom Gana Parishad
AIUDF	All-India United Democratic Front
APCC	Assam Pradesh Congress Committee (known as the Assam Provincial Congress Committee, pre-Independence)
BJP	Bharatiya Janata Party
BMS	Bharatiya Mazdoor Sangh
BPF	Bodoland People's Front
BTAD	Bodoland Territorial Areas District
ILP	Inner Line Permit
INTUC	Indian National Trade Union Congress
MLA	member of the Legislative Assembly
MP	member of Parliament
NDA	National Democratic Alliance
NEDA	North-East Democratic Alliance
RSS	Rashtriya Swayamsevak Sangh

SAG   South Asian Games
ULFA   United Liberation Front of Assam
UMF   United Minorities Front

FOREWORD

~

As a young Rashtriya Swayamsevak Sangh (RSS) activist, I would read and hear about two regions of the country very often—Jammu and Kashmir and the North-east of India. It was always in the context of activities of anti-national forces and terrorist groups in these regions and how they were posing a threat to India's territorial integrity. As I climbed up the ladder in the organization, I was able to better appreciate the challenges and threats from the region. I became a member of the drafting committee that would pass the resolutions during the annual national meets of the RSS, at least three on an average in a year. These resolutions highlight the ideological priorities of the organization and offer guidelines to the *swayamsevak*s to work towards the goals decided upon in the annual meetings. Not a single year passed without concerns being raised within the RSS over the issues in these regions.

Jammu and Kashmir was, of course, the dominant theme, but the North-east was not far behind. Over a period of a decade I have drafted at least four resolutions on various issues in the region, including on infiltration, border fencing, the

Chakmas, the Riangs, the United Liberation Front of Assam (ULFA) and on Naga issues. National-level responsibility in the organization has provided me the opportunity to visit the North-east several times. During one such visit, I even travelled to the remote Tripura–Mizoram border to meet about 50,000 Riang refugees who had been forced to flee their homes in Mizoram in the mid-1990s.

Coincidentally, when I joined the Bharatiya Janata Party (BJP) in 2014 and became its general secretary, the regions entrusted to me were Jammu and Kashmir and the North-east. The BJP had little or no presence in these areas. The North-east especially, with it extreme diversity, has always eluded a nationalist and integrationist party like the BJP. So the assignment was naturally challenging.

The North-east is geographically one region but it is hardly homogenous. Each state has its own peculiar characteristics. Within each state too one encounters vast diversity. Physical distance from the political capital of the country, a general neglect of and ignorance about the region are issues as well. One has to acknowledge and respect this diversity in order to succeed in influencing the people. I believe that grooming diverse local leadership is the key to success for any political party in this region.

One wishing to work in or for the North-east must learn to respect the diversity of this region. Even in the desire to look and sound 'national', one should not disrespect or discard this diversity and uniqueness. This one lesson helped us enormously when we faced the first election in Assam in early 2016. Of course, we had Modiji's popularity as a big weapon to use in the elections, but the political and economic conditions in the country at the time were not very encouraging for the BJP. The party had endured two successive defeats in the Delhi and Bihar assembly elections. It also did not have much presence in the states that were going to polls together along with Assam—Kerala, Tamil Nadu and West Bengal. There were other issues too that were working against the party then, such as the fact that dal was being sold in excess of Rs 200.

Yet, the BJP had been able to do exceedingly well in Assam and secured sixty seats in the 126-member assembly. Together with its allies, it had eighty-seven members, which is more than two-thirds majority. A BJP–Asom Gana Parishad (AGP)–Bodoland People's Front (BPF) coalition government led by Sarbananda Sonowal has since been put in place and is running the state successfully.

Looking back, I feel that two or three important factors helped us win this first major state in the North-east for the BJP. We were successful in forging a rainbow coalition with the AGP and the BPF, thereby giving the people a feeling that we were capable of unseating the fifteen-year-old Congress regime. The election was largely centred around local concerns, focusing on the misdeeds and failures of the Assam Congress government under chief minister Tarun Gogoi. We didn't allow the debate to turn to national issues. Projecting Sarbananda Sonowal, a soft-spoken tribal leader, as the chief ministerial candidate too helped us in a big way. The induction of Congress dissident Himanta Biswa Sarma, who enjoyed huge popularity and is known as an organizer and doer, was also a benefit. But most importantly, through the campaign, we did not make a single mistake that would have given the Congress any scope to gain political or electoral mileage.

After Assam, the BJP has succeeded in forming a government in Manipur too. The strategy adopted in this state was different because BJP was much weaker in Manipur than in Assam. Here, the division of votes helped BJP. Hence, we contested the elections independently and won enough seats to come to power with the help of our coalition parties.

Three years down the line, everything has changed. Four out of the eight North-eastern states have BJP or National Democratic Alliance (NDA) governments. The ruling party in Sikkim, the Sikkim Democratic Front, has friendly ties with the BJP. It is also a part of the newly formed North-East Democratic Alliance (NEDA). A region in which winning seemed a far cry until recently has now become a potential source of strength for the BJP. We aim to expand influence in the remaining three states too.

But behind this North-east push is a larger national agenda. The North-eastern states lack development, which has led to the sprouting of innumerable militant outfits. The region has also become a playground for our neighbours. It has also been a victim of some of the most serious national problems such as infiltration and terrorism. The rise of the BJP in this region will provide us an opportunity to effectively tackle these problems. Our governments in states like Assam, Manipur, Arunachal Pradesh and Nagaland have already been doing a lot of work in that direction.

The North-east also offers a huge opportunity for our nation, being surrounded by five countries—Nepal, Bhutan, China, Myanmar and Bangladesh. Although landlocked, the region can act as the land pivot in India's Act East Policy, which underlines India's geostrategic priorities to improve its diplomatic relations with the East Asian and South East Asian nations. It is the gateway to all of South East Asia and beyond. Exploiting this opportunity and developing this region as the Act East hub is one of the top priorities of our government at the Centre. Already, the Assam government has set up an Act East Corporation, the first of its kind in the country, to leverage this potential, which will be a win-win for all.

Rajat and Shubhrastha have been an integral part of our campaigns in the North-east in the electoral as well as developmental aspects. They played a key role in strategy and campaign during the elections in Assam and Manipur. Right now they are assisting the BJP governments in the region in their developmental objectives. They continue to work with us in our electoral campaigns in states such as Tripura, Meghalaya and Nagaland. They are well educated and trained, and have excellent insights into the region, along with the required skills in election management. Above all, they have humility and a knack to be invisible, the most important quality required for election management.

Their experiences in the region form the backdrop of this book and would be of immense value to those who wish to understand the present and future of not just the BJP in the North-east but also the North-east itself.

Ram Madhav,
National general secretary, BJP,
and director, India Foundation

INTRODUCTION

'There is nothing new in the world except the history you do not know.'

—Harry S. Truman

~

It was mid-March in the year 1671. Raja Chakradhwaja Singha was pacing up and down the corridors of the Ahom palace. Night had set a while ago. Far off on the horizon he could sense his sentries guarding the honour of the Ahoms with all their might. But for how long?

The Mughals had attacked the Ahoms in an attempt to invade the region. Fifteen times before this the Ahoms had resisted and pushed them back. Would they be able to drive them away this time as well? These questions raced through Chakradhwaja Singha's mind as he paced nervously. While he thought of the history of his land and the brave warriors of his kingdom, he couldn't help but think of his own legacy.

The Ahom kingdom was established in AD 1228 by a Tai prince Sukaphaa, who belonged to the modern-day Yunnan province of China. He crossed the difficult Patkai terrain and established his kingdom in the fertile Brahmaputra valley. At that time, smaller kingdoms such as Sutiya and Kachari had occupied the north and south banks of the Brahmaputra. The Ahoms expanded their kingdom through conquests over the other smaller rulers. For almost four centuries, they virtually had a free run in the region without the fear of any external aggression. It was only around the turn of the seventeenth century that they were forced into a conflict with the mighty Mughals under Emperor Shah Jahan.

Another small kingdom, called the Koch, or Kamata, was sandwiched between the Mughal empire on its west (stretching up to Bengal) and the Ahom kingdom on its east (extending up to Kamrup, or modern Guwahati). The Kochs acted as a buffer region between the Mughals and Ahoms. When the Mughals attacked and annexed the Koch territory, the Ahoms were dragged into a conflict with the former. This started a century-long military conflict between the two.

The Mughals attacked the Ahom kingdom a total of seventeen times. Barring a few years, they had never succeeded in ruling this part of India. In 1663, they made deep inroads into the Ahom empire and captured its capital in Garhgaon near modern-day Sibsagar. The Mughal forces were led by Mir Jumla, carrying Aurangzeb's banner, while the Ahoms were led by their king, Jaydhwaja Singha. After losing the capital, Jaydhwaja was forced into an embarrassing treaty with the Mughals. He had to offer his daughter to the imperial harem of Aurangzeb and also offer war bounties in form of gold, silver and elephants. The terms of the treaty were so unfair that the Ahoms decided to fight back and reclaim their lost territory, and above all, their lost glory.

As Chakradhwaja Singha recalled this past, he was overcome by anger and grief. This was the sixteenth time the Moghuls had come back to invade Assam. He remembered how his cousin, Jaydhwaja Singha, had fallen ill after being forced to sign the treaty and died soon after, before he could reorganize the Ahoms to fight.

Chakradhwaja Singha felt the weight of history on his shoulders. Under trying circumstances, he had had to take over the reins of the Ahom kingdom and rapidly work towards a reversal of fortunes. Thinking about the prospect of subordination to a foreign power made his blood boil.

Soldier after soldier was succumbing to the onslaught of the Mughal army. The Mughals, well versed in fighting on land and being commanded by Raja Ram Singh of Amber, had managed to do considerable damage to the Ahom army. Armed with grenades and new-style warfare, they were eager to finish off the Ahoms and claim Assam.

Chakradhwaja Singha could not decide who to put in charge of his mighty warrior race to lead from the front. Lost in deep reverie, he looked at the far end of the palace. The light from gigantic lamps flickered on the fort posts. He systematically went through each warrior in his mind. Each of them was fierce in his own right, but he couldn't pick out a leader from among them.

Lost in his thoughts, he stumbled as he walked up and down a palace corridor. But before he could fall, a sturdy arm helped him recover. The faint light from the palace revealed the visage of a young, handsome and fierce looking soldier of the Ahom army, Lachit Borphukan.

Son of the first Governor of Assam, Momai Tamuli Borbarua, a skilled and educated diplomat and principal Secretary to the Ahom kingdom, Lachit was a formidable warrior of the Ahom army. Trained in the know-how of guerrilla warfare, he had led several successful battles in the past. Most importantly, his hunger to succeed and not rest until the goal had been achieved made him an apt choice for the king. His scruples were apparent in that he had killed even his own kin on hearing of the latter's dereliction of duty.

Chakradhwaja Singha's eyes shone with hope. He heard Lachit narrate the reports of the day. On being asked about the preparation of the battle ahead, Lachit drew out an intricate plan to thwart the Mughals on land and divert them to the waters of the Brahmaputra, and explained the tactics to defeat them in the war. Chakradhwaja Singha asked Lachit to lead the mighty Ahom army, convinced that the general would ensure a glorious victory for the Ahoms.

The Mughals had been successful in claiming a major portion of their land in Guwahati. Seeing the sacred burial mounds of his ancestors being soaked in blood, Lachit felt the promise on his shoulders. He immediately sprang into action.

The soldiers were directed to not sleep even a wink till the war preparations were over. Lachit detailed the strategy of the war ahead and directed the Ahom soldiers to get the Mughals off the ground and draw them towards the banks of the Brahmaputra.

The Brahmaputra is so large that it is called a *nad* and not *nadi* in folklore. (The Brahmaputra river is named as the son of the creator of the cosmos, Brahma, in Hindu mythology. Most rivers in India are imagined and worshipped in the feminine form. But the Brahmaputra, because of its vast expanse and form, is considered masculine.) To choose where to fight the battle in the river was a strategic call. Lachit directed his army to lead the Mughals to a place called Saraighat, situated on the north bank of the Brahmaputra. The huge body of water, which is extremely wide, narrows down in Saraighat. This makes it an ideal ground for naval defence. This is the only place where the river's girth offers a unique vantage point to concentrate on enemy vessels and surprise them with a guerrilla attack.

What followed this move was a sequence of bitterly fought skirmishes between the resolute Ahoms and the equally determined Mughals. Finally, the Ahoms drove the latter to Saraighat. As soon as they succeeded in pushing back the Mughals to the water, the Mughal army fell like a pack of cards. They surrendered defeat and left Guwahati to the Ahoms, relinquishing their dream to have a foothold in the North-east.

This iconic war of 1671, famously known as the Battle of Saraighat, is etched in the imagination of Assam. Right from the theme of the war to the heroism of Lachit and the contemporary parallels drawn with the battle, it remains an emotional, cultural parable in Assam.

Other Battles of Saraighat

Commemorating Lachit's bravery, 24 November is celebrated in Assam as Lachit Divas. The Best Cadet of the National Defence Academy in Guwahati is conferred the Lachit Borphukan Gold Medal. And all this is done to honour the warrior's bravery and nationalism. But what did Lachit represent? Why do the Assamese get so sentimental about Lachit? And most importantly, what does the Battle of Saraighat mean to Assam?

The attack of the Mughals on Assam was seen as an attack on the historical, cultural and ethnic identity of the inhabitants—primarily the Ahoms, the ruling class. The idea of their ancestral lands being in the hands of aggressive outsiders or 'foreigners' was a terrible one for the culturally proud Ahoms. This battle was primarily fought to assert Ahom pride and culture and to preserve their heritage and legacy.

Not only does history celebrate the heroism of the Ahoms, politics too claims its fair share in the metaphor of this battle. The invocation of cultural pride is a reference that has pervaded the political consciousness of Assam in its more recent history. The question of Assamese identity and the resistance to be dominated by any force that is alien to its culture and history has been a vexed issue that has informed all major political upheavals in the state. And each of these times, the struggle of the Ahoms at Saraighat has been used as a parallel to draw inspiration.

During the Assam Movement (1979–85), the threat to the identity and cultural demography of the state was a palpable threat that nourished the sentiments of the protesters. The Battle of Saraighat remained a historical metaphor even then. Once foreign aggression began to be seen as a recurring phenomenon, political leaders started claiming the legacies of Sukaphaa and Lachit to assert their pure Assamese pedigree.

During the 2011 and 2016 assembly elections in Assam, illegal migration from Bangladesh remained at the heart of citizens' concerns. By 2016, the demography of the state had changed drastically. By calling the elections 'the Last Battle of Saraighat', the BJP evoked a complex history. The sense of urgency generated by calling it the last, the one and only, Battle of Saraighat against the demographic, cultural and political aggression of the illegal Bangladeshis threatening the essence of the state made this a people's movement.

However, this struggle of 'us versus them', 'insider versus outsider' is not just limited to Assam. If one analyses the basic emotion that drives people to so fondly remember and recount the Battle of Saraighat, one would realize that such battles are being fought across the landscape of the North-east. The struggle over crucial resources, the most scarce among them being land, has been a politically fraught issue for the entire region. In fact, the Balkanization of post-Independence Assam into smaller states of Nagaland, Meghalaya, Mizoram and Arunachal Pradesh was primarily the result of such a struggle. Even independent kingdoms like Manipur and Tripura are reeling under intercommunity rivalry.

Every community in the North-east is riddled with insecurities about the other. It seems they are entangled in a perpetual zero-sum game with each other. Pick the case of Manipur for instance. Three communities—the valley-based Hindu Meiteis; the hill-based, predominantly Christian Nagas; and the Kukis—inhabit Manipur. The state is shaped like a saucer, covered with hills on all sides and a valley in the centre. The fertile valley comprises just 8 per cent of the land area of the state. Naturally, if the hill tribes start settling there in large numbers, instances of xenophobia are likely to increase among the valley inhabitants—the Meiteis. It can be seen reflected in the very violent social movements both for and against the introduction of the Inner Line Permit (ILP) in Manipur.

The ILP is an official travel document issued by the Government of India to grant inward travel of an Indian citizen into a protected area for a limited period. It is obligatory for Indians residing outside those states to obtain special permission prior to entering the protected areas. The ILP regime is currently operational in Nagaland, Arunachal Pradesh and Mizoram—all three being tribal states of India. The deep-rooted insecurities of the Meiteis forced them to agitate in support of the ILP system. The leaders of the movement claimed that unabated migration from Myanmar and Bangladesh resulted in stress on their land and resources and therefore they wanted constitutional protection for the locals.

Similarly, in Arunachal Pradesh, the indigenous people still resist government doles to grant citizenship rights to the Chakmas. The Chakmas are mostly political refugees from erstwhile East Pakistan who settled in Arunachal Pradesh from 1964 to 1969. They now constitute a sizable population of fifty thousand—most of whom should have become Indian citizens by naturalization or birth. While their citizenship is politically contested by the local Arunachalis, the main issue remains that of land. Arunachalis strongly resist any attempt by non-locals to acquire the rights for owning land in the state that is protected by the ILP system. Any attempt at dilution of the ILP draws a sharp divide between the indigenous and non-indigenous communities—on similar lines of the 'us' versus 'them' theme—reminiscent of the Battle of Saraighat.

In our political assignments in different states of the region, we have grappled with similar factionalism. In societies that have been divided along the issue of identity there seems to be little or no margin for error. Our assignments, therefore, have a larger objective of avoiding fuelling the divide between 'micro' communities for political shortcuts. We have to ensure that we delicately weave together the parochial regional and community narratives into a cohesive national one, especially in the electoral narrative of the region.

The BJP's Tryst with the North-east

In an interview at the Ideas Exchange event hosted by the *Indian Express* in March 2016, then chief minister of Assam, Tarun Gogoi, was asked a question—'What is it about the North-east that makes it so important to the BJP?'

To that he said—'They want it all. They want to show that they are an all-India party.'

The BJP's desire to govern the entire North-east arises for obvious reasons. The party believes that for securing national integration, the border regions are the most critical. And they believe that for the fulfilment of the ideological vision of 'Akhand Bharat' and for the nation to be culturally and nationally integrated in spirit and not just geography, the North-east is crucial. For the BJP, it is not a peripheral state but the heart of India.

The sun rises earlier in North-eastern India than in the rest of the country. However, this region remained in 'darkness' for a very long time—darkness of vision, darkness of governance, darkness of separatist violence, but most importantly, the darkness of indifferent colonial, and later, national politics. The British considered the North-east region a 'buffer state'—one whose day-to-day governance need not be interfered with. While the British plan didn't succeed, the Congress party too lacked imagination and continued the same approach towards the governance of the region. As a result of the hands-off approach of the party, over the course of time, several socio-political issues that could have been solved in due course through mutual understanding and negotiations, through constructive communication and contact, have become intractable now.

The BJP, on the other hand, had a clearer political articulation for the North-east, the region being an inalienable part of Akhand Bharat—an entity not merely limited to the geographical contours of the Indian nation state. However, the party never had the political mandate to implement its vision. A little more than a year ago, in 2016, they had just a nominal political presence—five members of the Legislative Assembly (MLAs) in Assam, eleven in Arunachal Pradesh, five in Nagaland and two in Manipur.

However, within the last year, the region has seen a political revolution of sorts. Five out of the eight North-eastern states now have either a BJP-led government (Assam, Manipur, Arunachal Pradesh) or an NDA government (Nagaland and Sikkim). With the states of Meghalaya, Tripura and Mizoram due for elections in 2018, and with the initial trends coming from these states, the party's graph is all set to go further up.

There are multifarious dimensions to this political uprising. First, it is worth exploring why a national party like the BJP has become a preferred choice for the electorate despite a negligible presence of representatives and party workers. Second, there is a need to investigate if the emergence of the party in the region has sprung out of the utilitarian needs of these states to align with the Centre. Third, it is worthwhile to ponder if the constructed 'subnational' and 'anti-national' streak in the region is the buzzword of the past.

On 24 May 2016, for the first time, Assam, the gateway to the North-east, chose a BJP-led government in the state with a two-thirds majority. Almost a year later, on 15 March 2017, Manipur too chose a BJP-led government in its assembly elections. Both states opted to oust the Congress governments after giving their leaders—Tarun Gogoi and Okram Ibobi Singh—a chance for fifteen years straight.

While the BJP had a basic organizational presence in Assam, it was incomparable to the might of the Congress. The BJP, over the years, has maintained a 20–25 per cent vote share in the state, never enough to translate this vote share into number of seats in the assembly. However, it was only in the 2016 elections that it crossed the threshold and witnessed a thumping victory to make a permanent dent on the body politic of Assam. Going by the track record of almost negligible development by successive Congress regimes in Assam, the BJP emerged as a preferred alternative political party symbolizing hope, and swift and equitable development for the region, along with the trusted leadership of Prime Minister Narendra Modi. In Assam, the election was also fought on the rhetoric of the 'Last Battle of Saraighat'. The fast-changing demography and the scourge of illegal Bangladeshi migration dominated the politics during the election time. The BJP not just captured the narrative but also won the hearts of the Assamese people with its aggressive stance to resolve the issues.

Low-level development parameters were also the principle electoral issue in Manipur. Adding to that, a glaring trust deficit between various communities in the state had manifested itself in the violence-drowned days of the insurgency and subnational movements. The BJP ran a creative electoral campaign to wrest power from the Congress. In spite of negligible cadre strength, the party was able to exploit the anti-incumbency to its advantage.

The perception that the North-eastern states align with the political forces occupying the Centre is factually incorrect. Assam chose Tarun Gogoi in the 2001 elections even when BJP was in power at the Centre. Similarly, in 2002, in Manipur, Ibobi Singh wrested power from an alliance of local parties backed by a couple of BJP MLAs. Again the Centre couldn't come to their rescue. North-east has had a complex polity which cannot be reduced to a rule of thumb.

Both the central and the state units of the BJP have come to appreciate the vast nuances underlying the politics of the region and have put in extra focus to think locally in its decision-making. In the short span of the party's emergence in the region, it has shown political maturity in handling the vexed political issues.

For instance, Manipur has seen deep communal strife for decades. All communities—the Meiteis, the Nagas and the Kukis—have mutually strained relations due to several historical reasons. The entire state is fixed in a complex zero-sum game between various communities, as any gains for one community is seen to be at the cost of the other. In such a sensitive region, the state government's responsibility is to repose faith in the rule of law, take a just stand on these issues and, gradually, heal the wounds.

Only time will tell if the politics of the region is able to expand its horizon beyond the almost impervious chicken-neck corridor. And time will also tell if the BJP is able to utilize this opportunity to its ideological advantage beyond political expansion. The ethnic diversity of the region that comes with distinct challenges of linguistic, cultural, sartorial and religious identities—mostly in conflict with each other—is a unique opportunity for the BJP to try out alternative models of cohesion and integration, ignoring the erstwhile politics in the region. This is possible only if they are able to align the region with its ideological vision of India. Only then will it do justice to the core objective of its politics.

The BJP, being a truly representative national political party today, with its government in five out of eight North-eastern states, understands the sensitivity of the politics of the North-east. It respects the uniquely complex and delicate cultural and political worldview of the region and therefore enjoys an amicable relationship with several regional parties of the North-east. In order to strengthen itself and the local politics of the region, it collaborates with many of these regional parties in alliances. This coexistence is a sign of deep mutual trust and understanding, of forging bridges to achieve common objectives.

The primary objective of being and sustaining in politics is the pursuit of power. It is about gaining legitimate power and authority to be able to do things one wants. The BJP will fight the next assembly elections not just in Nagaland but in Tripura and Meghalaya as well. It will fight with all its force and will fight to win. And it is also clear that these political victories will never compromise on its core ideological idea of 'Nation First'.

In our course of various political campaigns in the North-east, we have seen a continuous evolution of the BJP. Seeing this metamorphosis would be a remarkable exercise for any student of Indian politics. Starting off as a party that had the politics of cow belt and Hindi heartland in its instincts, to becoming a truly national party that embodies mutually conflicting and competing ideas, the BJP has set itself on a steep learning curve.

An imploring question from an *Indian Express* journalist sums up this evolution, 'What do T. Thangzalam Haokip of Henglep, Vungzagin Valte of Thanlon, V. Hangkhanlian of Churachandpur, Samuel Jendai Kamei of Tamenglong and Nemcha Kipgen of Kanpokpi have in common? They are all tribals, members of the new Manipur assembly, elected on BJP tickets. More significantly, they are all Christians, and have been elected from constituencies where almost 99% voters are Christian. The elections in Manipur have dismantled the myth that the BJP is a party that belongs to and works only for Hindus.'

It is indeed no wonder that in a political party like the BJP that openly flaunts its Hindutva credentials, its North-east foot soldiers like to call it the Bharatiya Jesus Party! It is this natural yet seemingly strange assimilation of political articulations that makes electioneering for the party in this region so interesting.

While the BJP strengthens its foothold in the North-eastern region, it will have to go through ideological churning afresh. Its hitherto majoritarian outlook would need to give some political space to a 'minority darshan' or philosophy. The term 'minority' implies those small communities and tribes whose political expression gets sidelined with mainland India's obsession with Hindu–Muslim, secular–communal narratives. And in order to assimilate this viewpoint, the party really needs to have a vision for being a true representative of the people of the North-east who have blessed them with unprecedented electoral bounties. Issues like the beef ban will continuously implore the BJP leadership to dovetail two very contrasting viewpoints—respecting the customary food habits of the tribals in the North-east on the one hand and balancing the pressures emanating from the Hindu heartland to ban cow slaughter. How effectively the party leaders can take these challenging issues head-on will determine the future prospects of the party in the region. Through this book we have highlighted how the BJP has tried to navigate several such politically tricky situations.

The need to write this book arose because during our course of work in the region, we realized that a lot of literature is available on the North-east written by the inhabitants of the land. But very few 'outsiders' have written about the region, lesser so about its political affairs. The writing of this book has been a humble attempt to understand these states a bit more than our political assignments.

How the Media Saw the North-east

There is a narrative that competes with the regional reality of the North-east. The national media has shied away from investing resources and above all emotions to understand the region. Most of the well-off media outlets do not have full-time correspondents even in the capital cities of the North-east. All reportage is outsourced to stringers and a handful of regional experts or local journalists who have returned after detailed reporting stints in Delhi and other metropolitan media hubs.

We have to understand and appreciate the fact that an average middle-class Indian stacks his or her information crate about the nation through the consumption of media narratives. This also applies to how the North-east has been perceived by an average Indian. Even a cursory research of the mainstream media narrative dominating this region of the country will corroborate the claim that blood and gore define the representation of the North-east. Many journalists and intellectuals in these states share this opinion. The portrayal of this region as a battleground of extremist and insurgent forces does no justice to represent the complexity of the North-east.

The entire region comprises of more than four hundred small and big tribes—a social milieu unseen in any other part of the world. The derisive and reductive clubbing of the seven very different states in the clumsy summation of the term 'Seven Sisters' also does little to earmark the uniqueness of each of these diverse cultures. A collective failure to look at these facets of the region has contributed to an already existing sense of alienation among its people.

However, the media, as an institution, cannot alone be blamed. Various other supporting ecosystems have also failed to intellectually embrace the region and appreciate its complexities. In general, there has been a paucity of grounded commentators who can effectively narrate and discuss the North-east. Often, it appears that the 22-kilometre-wide chicken-neck corridor, also referred to as the Siliguri Corridor, which connects the North-east with the Indian mainland has gradually proved itself to be too narrow to connect the seven states with the rest of India.

Gradual and consistent relegation of the region to the margins of national imagination and consciousness has been a story of systematic neglect and casual treatment of this part of India by successive political dispensations, governments and other ideological establishments. Seven decades of history and three generations of unimaginative political leadership have collectively pushed the entire region into a whirlpool of absolute despondency. The result has been a sustained clamour for an identity independent from India by some ideologically motivated individuals and groups.

The rise of many extremist organizations challenging the sovereignty and integrity of the Indian state in the North-east has been a telling turn of events that have unfolded over the years of their indifferent profiling by the ruling political dispensations at the Centre. The Assam Movement rallied around the illegal migrants from Bangladesh and the threat to Assamese identity. The Naga Movement was an assertion of the Naga identity ever since the First World War. The Mizo Movement largely centred around the creation of a Mizo front that respects the autonomy and self-government of the Mizos as opposed to the ignorant and indifferent leadership of the central government. These movements and ideologies sustaining the uprisings have been rooted in the assertion of an identity not distinct from the Indian mainland but because of the slight faced by various groups for not being identified and respected by subsequent political dispensations at the Centre.

Various insurgent groups in the North-east such as the ULFA, National Democratic Front of Bodoland, National Socialist Council of Nagalim, Kuki National Army, Garo Liberation Front, Bru National Liberation Front, National Liberation Front of Tripura, Hmar People's Convention (Democratic), Zomi Revolutionary Army, All Tripura Tigers Force, Liberation Tigers of Arunachal, National Liberation Army of Arunachal, United Liberation Tigers of Arunachal, Revolutionary Army of Arunachal Pradesh, etc. rose, proliferated and reached a critical mass of supporters soon enough to dominate the political scene in the region. While some of these groups are still active, most of them had their heyday in the 1960s and 1970s. The violence that has ensued has completely blinded the political discourse of the region against their demands for autonomy or secession or sovereignty. But what has systematically been ignored is the fact that these insurgent organizations were byproducts of a larger political malaise, a reaction against a series of the irresponsible actions of the state.

Not only has our political system failed to fulfil the promise of nation-building and for creating a national consciousness for this part of the country, our education system, the media machinery and other ideological institutions have failed to integrate the mainland into the sociocultural moulds of North-east India. The lengthy and contrived corridors of Indian history writing, for instance, have systematically failed to cipher the heroism of Sukaphaa and Lachit Borphukan. It has failed to narrate the contributions of Srimanta Sankardeva and Azan Fakir. It never recognized Rani Gaidinliu, Paona Brajabashi, Tirot Sing Syiem, Khuangchera, Matmur Jamoh, Bir Tikendranath among so many others as part of the national curriculum and discourse while recounting the glorious faces of the Indian freedom struggle.

Assam: A Case Study

Assam was our first political assignment in the North-east. The gateway to the other states in the region and one that shares its international boundary with Bangladesh and Bhutan, it is a land of amazing diversity. Home to more than fifty tribes and identified as having a tripartite regional complexity, the social, political, ethnic and demographic character of Assam is a unique investigation in itself. The complexities and diverse hues of the state have prompted scholars to call it 'mini India'.[1] Our book focuses its primary attention on Assam and treats it as a sample case of understanding the politics in the North-east region. We have come to appreciate the fact that in order to work in the region, we need to understand and know the states as they are and not as they have been portrayed. We have come to know that we have to live and be here in order to work here.

The intercommunity rivalry between the various groups in Assam, the complex ethnographic politics of the Upper Assam and Barak Valley, often antagonistic to each other, the amazing linguistic and cultural diversity with each cultural entity asserting its uniqueness in the most mesmerizing way, the confluence of Shakti and Vaishnavite *parampara* alongside the tribal traditions of various groups—these and many more issues worth exploring—defined Assam for us.

This complexity is symptomatic of the issues in other states of the region as well. Therefore, the writing of this book was prompted by our urge to take the first step forward towards understanding the region. Assam is just a test case of our study. It is a template for us to approach and understand the other states in the region. This book is just a summation of what we have been able to gather so far.

In the life cycle of politics and ideologies, election campaigns are the most intense period. The electoral rhetoric and narrative used in the election campaign of Assam seemed like a quick revision of the region's history. Right from the beginning, BJP's Assam campaign was soaked in rich historical anecdotes. From resurrecting and venerating the historical icons of Assam like Sukaphaa, the first Ahom King, to Lachit Borphukan, the valiant Ahom general, the party ensured that it touched the emotional chord of people before even talking about politics and elections.

Through this book we have tried to put together our understanding of Assam gathered by being a part of our first election campaign in the North-east, by reading up on the history and politics of the region and by talking to countless experts and opinion makers in the state. Through this book we have also tried to work out an approach for investigating the other states in the region. This book is an exercise undertaken purely as a responsible Indian citizen who must know about one of the most unique and complex regions of the world.

~

On a balmy May evening, we strolled down the banks of the Brahmaputra river along the busy patch between Fancy Bazaar and Uzan Bazaar in Guwahati, just after concluding the election campaign. The cacophony of elections and its near miraculous results for the BJP had by then paled into recent history. The calmness of the mighty river stood in sharp contrast to the hectic months gone by.

Against the silhouette of the saffron sky and the golden rays of the setting sun dancing on the ripples of the Brahmaputra, a 35-feet-tall tall statue of Lachit Borphukan with his soldiers stood prominently in the middle of the torrential river. This statue represents the valour and pride intrinsic to Axomiya (loosely, 'Assamese') conscience that has fought external aggression within and outside Guwahati. It also represents the timelessness of concerns and the echoes of issues that has punctuated and defined the existence of Assam over centuries. And above all, it stands for the history unfolded, history being lived and history about to be made on the socio-spatial expanse of the state.

The seemingly calm yet ever-churning waters of the Brahmaputra flowed by as a perpetual witness to all that Assam had seen and will see in the epochs to come. As if letting go but still embracing Lachit Borphukan and his team of men in its womb, the Brahmaputra at Saraighat beckoned us to chronicle what was declared as the Last Battle of Saraighat in the rallying cry for the 2016 assembly elections.

29 September 2017

chapter one

A HISTORY OF POLITICAL BLUNDERS

'History has many cunning passages, contrived corridors
And issues, deceives with whispering ambitions,
Guides us by vanities.'

—'Gerontion' by T.S. Eliot

~

On 28 March 2016, in the early days of the campaign trail in Assam, BJP president, Amit Shah, took to the stage in a public rally in Lakhimpur amidst roars of 'Bharat Mata *ki jai*!' A little into his speech, he began with his scathing attack on the legacy of Congress policies in the North-east, most of which was the erstwhile Assam. 'Jawaharlal Nehru wanted Assam to be included in "D" [C] category states after Independence. But Mahatma Gandhi and Gopinath Bordoloi (the state's first chief minister intervened,' Shah told his audience.[1]

The response from the crowd gathered was deafening. Enthused by the cheers, Shah went on to build a strong counter-narrative of the failures of successive Congress regimes in the state, pointing out the historical blunders committed by Jawaharlal Nehru and his daughter, Indira Feroze Gandhi, vis-à-vis the issues in Assam, turning the heat on the Tarun Gogoi government and thereby projecting the BJP as a party that rightfully deserved a chance to serve the people of Assam.

The rest of India fights elections on the planks of development, caste combination, governance and corruption. Thus, it was peculiar to find an election run so passionately over claims of history and so steeped in the narratives of the political past. It became clearer with each passing day of the election cycle how recounting history in Assam was about remembering a series of political blunders by successive governments at the Centre and in the state. It was eye-opening to see how these mistakes have impregnated long-term implications on the psyche of the state. The enthusiastic response to historical facts being recalled were emblematic of the scars Assam conceals—scars that were inflicted upon the state by the ruling elite of Delhi.

It is therefore pertinent to recount some of the stark political blunders committed (or at best avoided) by India's central leadership, dominated by the Congress.

Assam's Little Nationalism

Assam has always been a land enriched by migrants. The gentry of the Brahmaputra valley used cheap labour from Bengal (now Bangladesh) to help them till their farms and engage in agriculture. Later, the British brought in cheap labour from tribes in Jharkhand to work on the tea estates. Much later, generations of professionals from various parts of India, as far as the south, settled in the North-eastern oil fields. Despite all this migration and settling down, why did the national consciousness never become central to the North-east identity?

Assam, a British province, had a relatively smooth accession to India. However, the weaving together of an Assamese identity co-terminus and integral to the larger Indian consciousness, was a task full of complications—largely glossed over by the leadership in Delhi. During the anti-colonial struggle, Assam was fighting two battles of independence simultaneously—one against the British colonial rule and second, against the Congress and the Muslim League.

The political consciousness awakened against the colonial rule did not just feed the anti-British struggle in Assam but also helped kindle a counter consciousness towards safeguarding the rights of the 'sons of the soil'[2] within Assam as well. This expression of unique selfhood within the Indian nationalist movement was by and large unnoticed and ignored by the national leaders.

The Assam Provincial Congress Committee (APCC, known as the Assam Pradesh Congress Committee after Independence), constituted in 1921 of former members of the Assam Association,[3] made an effort to oust the British colonial powers. It was also the much-needed buffer between the demands of a pan-Indian identity by the Indian national leaders and the growing aspirations of the Assamese middle-class intelligentsia. However, the mistrust remained and the Assamese nationalists referred to the APCC leadership as a 'rubber stamp' or 'gramophones' to push the agenda of their 'all-India bosses'.[4]

Snubbed by the cultural and political stalwarts from mainland India, two bodies—Assam Chatra Sanmilan and later the Assam Sahitya Sabha—became the 'lynchpin of nationalism in Assam'[5] through their advocacy for a 'Swadhin

Assam', meaning, a separate sovereign state. While there was no specific demand for an independent Assam, the expression of an independent identity against that of the mainstream was cautiously nursed by these organizations.

There were two important aspects of the expression of Swadhin Assam. First was the raw sentiment of emotional attachment towards the Assamese language among the people of the state and, second, the palpable insecurity of losing the language and its cultural expressions, precipitated through uncontrolled infiltration of Bengali from the physical migration from East Bengal to Assam.

Both these issues received just a passing remark from the national leaders during the Independence movement. Thus, the collective angst of the Assamese against the mainland leaders of the Congress on such a delicate issue was nurtured over the years preceding India's independence.

'The fear of being inundated and overtaken by "stronger" nationalities was attempted to be confronted by a sustained stress on separate identity of Assamese people . . .'[6] New dictums like 'India is the Mahadesh of the Indian Mahajati' and 'Assam for Assamese'[7] were doing the rounds in the local Assamese press. A section of the intelligentsia appealed to Nehru, who was visiting Rongia in November 1937: 'As a means of saving the Assamese race [from] extinction a considerable section of the Assamese intelligentsia has even expressed their minds in favour of the secession of Assam from India.'[8] Nehru ignored this sentiment. He instead blamed it on the parochialism of the Assamese opinion makers. In the intervening years, the clamour for 'Assam deciding its own fate' did not die. On 17 July 1947, the *Assam Tribune*, a popular daily, reported that Assam Jatiya Mahasabha suggested transferring a part of the erstwhile Goalpara district, the chief link of the state with mainland India through the 'chicken neck', to East Pakistan in the making. This would have geographically cut off Assam from the rest of India and given it an independence that was viable to form a sovereign nation.

As if continuing with the practice of not paying heed to the concerns and uniqueness of the North-east, the national anthem[9] of India, first scripted in 1911, ignored mention of the North-east completely. While Indianness was being richly articulated through songs and symbols in the national anthem during the freedom struggle, much to the ignominy of India's composite culture, not even one of the seven states or any of their reference found mention in the anthem. Assam's culture-conscious strata vehemently opposed the anthem when it was aired on the All India Radio station in July 1948.

An omission of a region from the national anthem in a country as complex as India has the potential to significantly impact the psyche of the people. This historical blunder committed by Rabindranath Tagore is considered one of the reasons for the animosity between Bengalis and Assamese scholars[10] besides being touted as a justification for Assam's identity politics.

Though the extreme notions of Swadhin Assam remained limited to the imagination of only a few, the pain and hurt of this more universal slight never healed. The economic non-viability of the idea of separation made it a non-starter, but the sociopolitical ramifications of it have haunted the national scenario for a long time. Overall, the unsympathetic attitude of the default political establishment led by the Congress towards dealing with the vexed existential issues facing Assam allowed the initial seeds of separatism to germinate in the soils of the Brahmaputra.

Despite the cultural convergence of the Indian and Assamese realities, the national political manifestation failed to reflect the Assamese aspirations and expectations as part of the national selfhood.

The Great Betrayal

Gopinath Bordoloi was an individual stuck at the crossroads of two nationalist ideas—one of India and the other of Assam. Bordoloi was the Prime Minister of Assam (before the promulgation of the Constitution of India, the chief minister of a province was called the 'prime minister') from September 1938 to November 1939 and again from February 1946 until his death in August 1950. He is perhaps best remembered in India for his relentless opposition to the Cabinet Mission's grouping proposal of 1946 and his efforts towards preventing Assam from sliding into the hands of Pakistan. It is a less popular yet an interesting story to learn how a pragmatic politician and a true Gandhian, Bordoloi single-handedly ensured the failure of the ill-conceived Cabinet Mission Plan.

In 1940, several prominent APCC members were jailed for their opposition to the British imposition of the Second World War on India. Gopinath Bordoloi, Fakhruddin Ali Ahmed, Bishnu Ram Medhi, Gauri Kant Talukdar, Lakeshwar Barooah and Debeshwar Sarma were among those jailed. In the Jorhat jail, they conducted what was called the 'Bordoloi's Nation-Building Meetings'. The meetings were designed to discuss the future territorial boundaries of Assam, its relationship with frontier areas and Manipur and Assam's internal problems and solutions. They also deliberated on Assam's own nationalism.

Another individual nursing a parallel vision of a possible third nationality in the region was Sir Saiyid Muhammad Sadullah. Sadullah was a prominent Assamese leader representing the Muslim League in the Assam assembly. He was also the Prime Minister of Assam from 1939 to 1946. An ethnic Assamese Muslim, he strove for a Greater East Pakistan, including Assam in its fold. He served as the principal political and ideological opposition to Bordoloi and Congress leadership in the state.

In the ideological tussle that ensued between the Congress and the Muslim League, Sylhet, a small town in erstwhile southern Assam became the fulcrum of politics in Assam. The demography of Sylhet, with its majority of Muslims, became an identity marker for the state, leading to a broad perception of Assam in the rest of the country as that of a Muslim-majority state. Bordoloi lamented, 'There is no one [in Assam] to explain to the general mass of Indians that Assam is not a state to be incorporated into the League's concept of Pakistan.'[11] Sadullah exploited this confusion in the minds of national leaders regarding Assam and used it to craft a new demand for a Muslim nationality. Jinnah and the provincial Muslim League leaders aspired for the whole of Assam to be included into East Bengal and to make Shillong their summer resort capital.

The deep differences between India's interests as articulated by the national leaders, the Assamese interests led by the APCC leaders and the Muslim League interests led by Sadullah came to the forefront in 1946. After nearly two months of rigorous deliberations, the Cabinet Mission announced its plan on 16 May 1946. The plan envisaged a 'Union of India' consisting of various provinces or units, which would have full autonomy and keep with them all residuary powers except in matters of external affairs, defence and communication. These general provisions were much to the pleasure of those who wanted the sovereignty to rest in the hands of a provincial government.

However, the principle deal-breaker was the 'Grouping' provision introduced in the Cabinet Mission Plan. The Plan envisaged a three-tier Constitution structure—the Centre, the group and the province. The provinces of India were to be divided into three groups or sections—A, B and C. The six Muslim-dominated provinces were constituted in sections B and C. Section C (the same one Amit Shah mentioned in his speech) included Bengal and Assam. By virtue of this classification, Assam was deemed to be a state in the Muslim-dominated region. The Cabinet Mission Plan drew a silhouette of the future East Pakistan, and left citizens in the state wondering if they would become part of this region.

According to Nirode Barooah, 'The problem with Assam was that since this Hindu majority province would be together with the Muslim predominated Bengal in one Section, the acceptance to the Section would automatically mean opting for the Group and getting thereby submerged in Bengal. In fact, there can be no doubt that the grouping provision was especially made to satisfy the Muslim League.'[12] Barooah further stated that instead of conceding to the demand of 'Pakistan' as such, this Grouping Plan was conceived as a 'halfway house' such that two Muslim-dominated areas would emerge to represent the notion of a 'Muslim nation'.

The Grouping provision was antithetical to the very existence of Assamese nationality. With one stroke, any simmering of the idea of a sovereign Assam was put to rest. In the light of the machinations of the Muslim League to include Assam in East Pakistan, the people of Assam emotionally backed the Congress and its politics. In spite of the popular support, the Congress, in its attempt to appease the Muslim League and find a hurried solution to India's independence agreed to the Cabinet Mission Plan. The All India Muslim League also accepted the Plan, declaring that the 'germ and essence of Pakistan was there'.[13] In the hurry to create new nationalities, Assam's interests were betrayed.

Trying to save itself from this plan became yet another struggle for Assam within its demand for independence. The reactions of the central Congress leaders, especially Nehru and Maulana Abul Kalam Azad, on the demands of Assam were carefully scrutinized by the people of Assam and its press. While Nehru was initially sympathetic to Assam's reservations against the Grouping Plan and advocated the resolution to be passed against the Grouping provision, he also believed that such controversial issues might be easily dealt with within the Constituent Assembly.

Meanwhile, as the head of the provincial government, Bordoloi 'moved a mandatory motion in the Assam assembly directing its ten members in the Constituent Assembly to not sit with the Bengal representatives while deliberating on Assam's Constitution'.[14] He firmly stood behind the rights of the Provinces to frame their own constitutions.

Due to a lack of understanding with the Congress on the issue of an interim government, the Muslim League eventually withdrew from the Cabinet Mission, resulting in the call to Direct Action on 16 August 1946. Nehru's hopes of settling all contentious issues at the Constituent Assembly, where the Congress secured an overwhelming majority, could not be realized. The insecurity of the Muslim League at being outnumbered by the Congress in the assembly is what led them to carry out a complete boycott.

During the impasse on the Cabinet Mission Plan, Nehru, Baldev Singh, Jinnah and Liaquat Ali Khan were called to London. On 6 December 1946, the British government stated clearly that 'Cabinet Mission's Plan was an indivisible whole and no party could accept a part of it and reject the other'.[15] Furthermore, each contentious issue was to be decided in the Sections by a simple majority of votes. This was referred to as the 6 December Statement.

The 6 December Statement further crystallized the grouping provision, thereby resulting in utter dismay for Assam, which hoped to find a way out of the mess. Sensing betrayal at the hands of their own leaders, the APCC submitted another memorandum to the Congress Working Committee. Congress leaders from Assam realized that 'as time went by, even second-ranking All-India Congress leaders had little time to spare for them'.[16] No one higher up in the ranks of the Congress leadership showed any interest in the immediate problem of Assam, which would later prove to be a long-term issue.

At every crucial moment in his political and personal life, Bordoloi looked up to Gandhiji for solace and solution, and it was no different in this situation as well. Sensing complete indifference from the Congress leadership, Bordoloi sent out two emissaries, Bijoy Chandra Bhagwati and Mahendra

Mohan Chowdhury, to enlist Bapu's support in preventing Assam from becoming a part of Pakistan. Gandhiji's advice was categorical:[17]

> [I]f there is no clear guidance from the Congress Working Committee, Assam should not go into the Sections . . . As soon as the time comes for Constituent Assembly to go into Section, you will say, 'Gentlemen, Assam retires.' It will be a kind of Satyagraha against the Congress for the good of the Congress . . . If you don't act correctly and now, Assam will be finished . . . Assam must not lose its soul. It must uphold it against the whole world. Else, I will say that Assam had only manikins and no men . . .

In spite of Gandhiji's much needed vision for Assam, both Nehru and Azad thought that 'Assam's stand was helping the Muslim League and also acting as an obstruction to freedom'.[18] Nehru, while speaking to a Bengali delegation stated: 'Assam cannot hold up the progress of the rest of India and support to Assam would mean refusal to accept the British prime minister's statement of 6 December and letting loose the forces of chaos and civil war.'[19]

On hearing of Nehru's great betrayal and acceptance of the 6 December Statement, the people of Assam felt a sense of disillusionment with the central leadership and rebelled against the Congress with a vigorous Anti-Grouping Movement.

Meanwhile, the Provincial Muslim League upped its ante when it saw a glimmer of a chance of Assam's possible inclusion in its Pakistan project. When the Assam government, led by

Bordoloi, planned to evict illegal land encroachers from the state, the League saw it as a measure to evict Muslims from the region. Jinnah himself visited Guwahati in 1946 to protest against the eviction policy and virtually threatened: 'If the government does not immediately revise its policy and abandon this persecution, a situation will be created which will not be conducive for the people of Assam.'[20]

The idea of Pakistan was brought to the public imagination through various public meetings, especially during the celebrations of Pakistan Day on 23 March 1947. Slogans such as 'Larke Lenge Pakistan' echoed in the streets of Guwahati.[21] The spirit seemed to be reinforced by the lackadaisical and confused attitude of central Congress leaders, who seemed to have nothing to offer to placate the situation.

Seeing the impasse, the British government withdrew the Cabinet Mission Plan and replaced it with the Mountbatten Plan in 1947. The Mountbatten Plan did away with the entire grouping provisions and instead proposed the simplistic two-nation theory with the division of Punjab and Bengal on a communal basis. This also provided the framework for ceding of the Muslim-majority Sylhet district to the future East Pakistan. Eventually, Sylhet, through plebiscite, went to Pakistan and Assam, being a British ruled non-Muslim majority province, was allocated straightaway to the Indian Dominion. This ended Assam's decade-long struggle.

Fast forward to almost seven decades later, when Amit Shah at an election rally in Lakhimpur blamed Nehru for pushing Assam to 'Section D',[22] The spirit seemed to be reinforced was actually referring to Assam being pushed to Section C. He further elaborated how it was Gandhi and

Bordoloi who salvaged Assam from the situation. Amidst roars from BJP's Assamese supporters, Shah pointed out the grave historic blunder under the leadership of the Congress that almost led to Assam becoming a part of Pakistan.

This seemingly obtuse historical reference from Amit Shah at a political rally was not without a firm conviction of ideas. Not only has the BJP understood the politics of Assam from the prism of Akhand Bharat, it has also remained cognizant of the historical political follies. It is, therefore, not a matter of chance that the BJP, after coming to power at the Centre in 1998, conferred its very first Bharat Ratna—the country's highest civilian honour—to Gopinath Bordoloi, a seemingly political adversary of the BJP and a forgotten hero.

By doing so, the then prime minister Atal Bihari Vajpayee had not just revered a politician from the Congress, he had conferred respect upon a historic personality who had ensured that the ancient land of Pragjyotishpur remained with India. It is important to ponder why this realization never dawned on the Congress despite being in power for fifty long years.

Bordoloi had once famously said, 'He [Jinnah] might as well expect the moon come down to him but could never have Assam in his Pakistan.'[23] Such was the steely resolve of Bordoloi that ensured Assam stayed with India. The Bharat Ratna was indeed a befitting tribute to an epochal leader of India.

The Migration Conundrum

A national culture of indifference towards the issues of North-east had systematically ossified over time. While the entire country was horrified at the massacre that followed the partition of Punjab, the country hardly cared at that time about the looming refugee crisis and demographic shift taking place at its North-eastern front. No other issue in the last seventy years has vitiated the political climate of Assam more than the immigration problem. For the last seven decades, every single assembly election from the Provincial Elections of 1946 to the recently concluded elections in 2016, the only substantive electoral plank has been the uncontrolled illegal migrants into the state of Assam. Political parties, across the spectrum, have raked the emotive appeal of the issue to their parochial advantages. However, soon after the elections, the issue loses steam. The Assamese people had been voting for a party that sounded more convincing about giving assurances about preventing infiltration but abandoned the issue every single time.

The immigration problem has three dimensions—language, religion and resources, especially land.[24] The migration problem began predominantly in the context of the Assamese employing cheap labour from the surrounding regions to work in their farms and tea estates from around the late nineteenth century. Gradually, migrants looking for job prospects were naturally attracted to the valley. 'The Muslim migrants were cultivators in general, and they wanted land. But the Hindu immigrants, residing mainly in towns, were always after jobs and educational facilities for their children. They began to consider the Assam Valley, where they took up jobs or petty business as bilingual, and were keen to preserve Bengali as a medium of instruction for their children . . . This was against the unilingual concept of the Assam Valley . . . it was in anticipation of such a challenge . . . that the idea of secession of Assam from India was then being mooted by a section of Assamese intelligentsia.'[25]

Sir Saiyid Sadullah, the Premier of Assam from 1937–46, was accused of facilitating the first wave of mass Muslim migration into Assam from East Bengal. The massive famine that struck Bengal resulted in a mass exodus of people to the neighbouring province of Assam. In order to provide settlement to these fresh immigrants, the Assam government led by Sadullah adopted a resolution in 1943 called Grow More Food. 'The resolution provided for opening the grazing reserves in Kamrup, Darrang and Nagaon districts [in Central Assam] to land-hungry immigrant cultivators from Bengal'. Viceroy Lord Wavell interpreted it famously as 'Grow More Muslims'.[26]

Inner Line Regulation was a policy promulgated by the British in 1876 to keep the hill tribes of the North-east isolated from the plains of erstwhile Assam to safeguard their culture and way of life from the influx of outsiders. Over a period of time, and peaking around the 1940s, the clamour to extend the Line Permit System to the Assam plains took serious shape. The reason was that the permit system was thought of as a surrogate way of stopping Muslim immigration into the state. Neither the central Congress nor the Muslim League supported this proposal, the latter being vehemently opposed to it. The League also contemplated a mass civil-disobedience movement against any attempt to impose the Line System in the plain areas of Assam. Eventually, the Line Permit System remained a non-starter in the plains of the North-east, while the hills enjoyed the protection of the resources offered by this system.

The porous nature of the Bangladesh–Assam border allowed unabated migration for the next several decades. The degree of porosity of the borders can be understood by that fact that the chief secretary of East Pakistan and his family would

come to the resort city of Shillong without any documentation
or permission. No one could guess if it was merely for leisure
or a front for espionage. When Bordoloi raised the issue
with Nehru, his response was, 'We do not object normally to
particular person visiting India from Pakistan.'[27]

By 1949, Assam had already taken in more than 3 lakh
Partition refugees. The migration from East Pakistan continued
and the number of Bengali Hindu refugees increased from
2,73,000 in 1951 to 6,28,000 in 1961. According to the Census
of India report, the growth rate of Assam's population during
the 1950s was almost 35 per cent compared to the decadal
growth rate of 25 per cent for the rest of India. Put this in
context with the current migration into the Western countries:
accommodating even a few thousand refugees has wreaked
havoc on these countries, and toppled governments and global
political paradigms. Not anticipating a popular reaction from
Assam was politically naive and proved to be a huge blunder on
the part of its politicians.

Nehru's Sledgehammer Approach

Nehru had deep misconceptions about Assam and was therefore
less sympathetic towards Assam's chronic problems. Bordoloi, in
spite of his national stature, was unable to instil confidence in
Nehru. The latter doubted Bordoloi's judgement and 'showed
little respect' or a 'proper sense of dignity and balance' for his
compatriot.[28] Bordoloi faced the twin problems of this massive
influx of immigrants and a severe paucity of funds and land to
settle them. Instead of addressing the issue, Nehru retorted by
linking state grants to refugee settlement: 'Assam could expect

central financial help only if it liberally accepted refugees from East Bengal and granted them lands.'[29] Even on the land issue, Nehru doubted the seriousness of paucity of land in Assam: 'You say there is no further land available in Assam . . . if land is not available in Assam, it is still less available in the rest of India.' He went on to say, 'If Assam adopts an attitude of incapacity to help solve the refugee problem, then the claims of Assam for financial help obviously suffer . . . If Assam wants to follow narrow provincial policy excluding others, there are bound to be reactions against Assam in other parts of India. It will be difficult for the central government to have any major scheme in Assam.'[30]

Bordoloi, who held Nehru in reverence, was taken aback at the outburst meted to him. He believed that Nehru's views about Assam were coloured by the propaganda of the influential Bengali media, especially in fuelling the rumour that Assam demanded dual citizenship. In an uncharacteristically stern letter Bordoloi replied to Nehru, 'If some crank ventilate . . . the blame should neither go to the people of Assam nor to the government . . . I indeed feel greatly dismayed, when I find that much of these exaggerated and false propaganda against Assamese are believed by persons in authority because they have the support of the powerful press and can obtain contact at all levels in the rest of India. I am only sorry that you seem also to feel that Assam wants to follow a narrow provincial policy.'[31]

Nirode Barooah's work seems to suggest that Nehru trusted his intelligence officials to be his eyes and ears on Assam's matters more than the elected representatives of the state.[32] He apparently defied the basics of federalism when it came to handling the peculiar problems of the state. Barooah even went on to claim that Nehru adopted tough arm-twisting measures to force the state to toe Delhi's line. In a way, the serious issue of illegal migration was pushed down the timeline to be addressed at a later day.

One can empathize with Nehru who, at that time, was bogged down by the monumental task of building a nation—brick by brick and person by person. And this is exactly the reason why people from all over the country, especially the border regions such as the North-east, expected enormous commitment and perseverance from him. It is natural then that one feels let down by Nehru for not attributing primacy to issues pertaining to Assam.

Goodbye Assam

According to the *Times of India*, in his address to the nation on All India Radio on 20 November 1962, during the war with China, Nehru had said, 'Huge Chinese armies have been marching in the northern part of NEFA. We have had reverses at Walong, Se La and today Bomdila, a small town in NEFA, has also fallen. We shall not rest till the invader goes out of India or is pushed out. I want to make that clear to all of you, and, especially our countrymen in Assam, to whom our heart goes out at this moment.'

Surprisingly what was interpreted of it by the terrified masses was that during the 1962 Sino–Indian war, when the Chinese forces advanced up to Bomdila in Arunachal Pradesh, Nehru said, 'goodbye Assam'. This anecdote is oft recounted in the popular imagination of Assam as the lowest watermark of the Indian morale.

Upon hearing the prime minister say, 'My heart goes out to the people of Assam', a wave of panic swept across Tezpur, a town on the banks of the river Brahmaputra. After Bomdila—about 150 km from Tezpur—had fallen to the Chinese, there was every possibility that the Chinese army could be heading towards Tezpur. Thousands left hearth and home in Tezpur to flee south across the Brahmaputra. Guwahati was flooded with thousands of such refugees. Nonetheless, at midnight on 21 November 1962, China abruptly declared ceasefire. Yet, the fear of foreign occupation was such that people continued to flee their homes even after a unilateral ceasefire.

While serving in public office, communication plays a key role in connecting the people with the leader. And communication entails what people hear and not necessarily what the leader says. Though one might want to argue that Nehru's words '[M]y heart goes out to the people of Assam' were a genuine expression of pain and hurt, the words were received negatively by the people in Assam. No one has a clear answer as to why this twisted interpretation of Nehru's speech condensed in people's minds and stayed with them for decades.

Jawaharlal Nehru's speech continues to stoke the flames in Assam even today. Many in Assam continue to believe that Nehru was indifferent to the state. This speech made the people of Assam feel abandoned. It was like they were let down by their own government. At a time when even the prime minister seemed helpless, what was going to be their fate? The instance is brooded upon to reckon the Centre's seal of exclusionary stance towards the region. According to Prof. Nani Gopal Mahanta, 'This incident played a very proactive role in popularizing the secessionist thought among the new generations in the 1980s who believed that India had already left Assam and abdicated its responsibility to protect its own people.'[33]

As argued by some eminent journalists in Assam, Bhupen Hazarika's song 'Buku Hoom Hoom Kare' was an expression of the raw sentiments of the people of Assam in the wake of the Chinese aggression in 1962 and what they felt when Nehru reacted to the incident. An immortalized poet, journalist, artist and musician, Bhupen-da's song directly addresses Axomi Aai ('the motherland Assam') and narrates the cry of a helpless son calling out to his mother and resigning himself to the fate that awaits Assam. The feeling of the mother slipping away into darkness and the heart fluttering with a premonition was a palpably felt sentiment in Assam.

Memories of life, social and political, in the nascent nation did not bring about a sense of security and unity to the people residing in this periphery, which was already struggling with economic and developmental crisis. What the people of Assam needed then was a healing touch and sturdy support from the central leadership in Delhi, an assurance that all will be well and that they would be taken care of. What they felt instead was that they got a response bordering on indifference. What they received was an expression which essentially meant that Nehru was helpless, sad and heartbroken that Assam was slipping from Indian hands. Instead of dedicating some moments of grief and trying to boost up the morale of the people, as any statesman and leader of the nation would do, what Nehru should have said and done was far in contrast to what he ended up saying and doing. 'The main promises of India's nation-building—political participation, equal treatment before the law and protection from the arbitrariness of state power, dignity for the weak and poor, and social justice and security—were apparently not met in the case of Assam.'[34]

This incident is etched in the minds of the people of Assam. In fact, their support for the Congress has been because of an incidental vacuum in the political space of Assam and not necessarily because they see Congress as their representative. That is why in 1985, in the aftermath of the Assam Movement, Assam decisively overthrew the Congress at seeing a political opportunity. Similarly, in 2016, the people returned a decisive mandate and installed the BJP in their state assembly.

Writing on the Wall

Due to the centralizing features of the newly promulgated Constitution, the state government was never allowed to play any major role in critical policy making pertaining to the state. The new Constitution had decisively tipped the balance away from the provinces and put the residuary powers in the hands of the Centre. This precipitated into a culture where the central supremacy on legislative powers was also mirrored in their day-to-day dealing with the state. While the province-specific issues were being deliberated at the Constituent Assembly, the central leaders used to think of themselves as more 'all-India minded' than their provincial counterparts. The discussions, it seemed, were more to lend a patronizing ear to the provinces than actually being willing to hear and understand the issues as was the case in Assam. Nirode Barooah summarizes it succinctly: 'On many occasions, the Union leaders claimed superior understanding of the local situation and were determined to impose their will on the Bordoloi government.'[35] The two pillars of the Congress, Nehru and Sardar Patel, were both infected with this malaise. In order to portray an image of being neutral and India-minded, they became prisoners of their own image. The political–constitutional culture perpetuated by them, instead of solving, exacerbated the problems of newly created provinces in independent India. The high-handedness of the second rung Union ministers too on provincial stalwarts led to policy divergence and huge mistrust in issues critical to India's stability in its turbulent times. On their part, the central leaders too felt that provincial leadership acted as if they had the monopoly of truth and the Union government did not know their business.

Also, national leaders, who had much larger and wider issues to discuss, positioned the very act of giving a platform to the problems of Assam as an act of greatness. This patronizing and high-handed attitude of the Congress party reflected in general the way Assam was received in public imagination. This institutional stepbrotherly attitude is mirrored in the perception of Indians about the North-east in general. This, unfortunately, has perpetuated over generations.

In the subsequent decades, Assam witnessed all the above political blunders replayed in slow, agonizing, sustained and violent public movements in the form of the Language Movement in 1960, Refinery Movement in 1967, Movement on the issue of Medium of Instruction in 1972 and Anti-foreigner Movement in the early 1980s. Those who do not learn history are doomed to repeat it. India and its political leadership had clearly failed to learn anything from Assam's initial hiccups. Every historical blunder was richly recounted at the altar of the 2016 assembly campaign.

chapter two

THE RUN-UP TO THE 2016 ELECTIONS

'When our elephant [election symbol of the AGP] wakes up, it runs over all that comes in its way—it has already chewed up your hand [election symbol of the Congress].'

—Slogan by AGP supporters in the 1985 elections

~

Any election cycle witnesses at least a year-long intense focused campaign effort. Alliance questions, co-option of leaders, macro and micro strategies, communication, cadre and volunteer management, and selection of leaders are some key areas that require consistent work and attention over a period of time. What happened in Assam in 2016 was the result of meticulous planning, careful and consistent groundwork and of course, a creative campaign strategy. As depicted in the previous chapter, a campaign that seems rigorously fought over the span of a few months usually has much deeper and arduous background work and references to a political history of many years before the election. In case of the Assam elections, the foundation for BJP's stupendous win in the 2016 assembly elections was laid almost three decades ago, when the first seeds of an alternative ideology were sown in the Brahmaputra valley.

In the 1970s, the Congress was toying with various ideas to control the restive mood of the population. However, each time it came to electoral priorities it went back to a simplistic vote-bank centred strategy. In March 1977, there were 5,60,297 registered voters in the Mangaldoi Lok Sabha constituency of Assam. It was among the few seats that the Janata Party movement had managed to wrest from Indira Gandhi's Congress party, which had won ten of the fourteen Lok Sabha seats in the state, contrary to the Janata Party wave breezing across India. Almost exactly a year later when Hiralal Patowary, the sitting Janata Party member of Parliament (MP), passed away, the Election Commission of India was forced to conduct a bypoll for the Mangaldoi Lok Sabha seat. Within the span of this one year, defying all demographic logic, the total number of the electorate in Mangaldoi had increased by a whopping 80,000 voters. Essentially, about 15 per cent more people had miraculously appeared almost overnight in the area. Having lost the seat in 1977, the Congress 'imported' nearly 70,000 Bangladeshi Muslim refugees into Mangaldoi purely for electoral gains. Various citizen groups filed court cases against this import of voters. More than 70,000 cases were put under scrutiny to verify the authenticity of these voters. Of those cases, 26,900 were sustained. With this, the term 'illegal Bangladeshis' entered the lexicon of Indian politics. This term implied a euphemism to signify politically imported Bangladeshi Muslims.[1]

Illegal Migrants

While the estimate of the total number of illegal migrants in Assam has never been agreed upon, the civil societies projected the number to be between 4.5 to 5 million i.e. 31 to 34 per cent of the total population of the state in 1971.[2] There have been two big waves of refugee influx in Assam—first during the time of Partition in 1947 and second during the time of Bangladeshi War of Independence in 1971. Even in the interim years, the state saw a continuous stream of politically victimized minorities, especially the Bengali-speaking Hindus from East Pakistan coming into and settling down in the Brahmaputra valley.

The humanitarian obligation to accept them as political refugees was large heartedly identified by the Assamese. However, the Indian citizenship laws were not ready for the naturalization of such a large scale of migrants. The Constitution of India initially fixed 19 July 1948 as the deadline for migrants to claim Indian citizenship. Due to riots that broke out across, this date was shifted to 31 December 1951. While the exchange of population was considered final on the western boundary in Punjab on the given date, the eastern boundary in Assam and Bengal remained porous for several years.

The Muslim migrants from East Pakistan were mostly landless economic refugees. They found empty patches of land along the Brahmaputra riverine belt and settled there. 'Used to an amphibious mode of living and industry, these immigrants came by rail, streamers and bits up the Brahmaputra to reclaim those malarial areas. All they wanted was land. From their riverine base, they further pressed themselves forward in all directions in search of living space . . . it was then that an open clash of interests began to take place.'[3]

On the other hand, the Bengali Hindu refugees were people who had fled for mostly political reasons, and not economic ones. They were refugees from East Pakistan who were ostracized in their native lands. They were largely from the Sylhet district, which became a part of Pakistan at the time of Independence, and they migrated to the adjoining areas of Barak valley, such as Karimganj, Hailakandi and Cachar.

The difference between a legal citizen of India and an illegal migrant is a matter of a few identity documents that could be easily managed in those days of lax scrutiny. Ironically, migrants had far more detailed documentation to prove their roots in Assam than even the indigenous Assamese. With the passage of time, the problem of identifying migrants became increasingly difficult. Another crucial issue that needed to be settled was that of the 'cut-off date'—migrants who arrived before this date would be considered naturalized legal citizens. Those migrating after this date would be considered foreigners and would be deported. On the micro level, the alarming change in Assamese demography due to the influx of Bengali migrants had created a deep sense of insecurity in the minds of the Assamese. On the macro level, details such as setting the cut-off date and the definition of illegal migrants were being vehemently debated in the public arena. All such dimensions surrounding the deeply complex issue of immigration coalesced together into the Assam Movement, one of the largest public mobilizations India had ever seen.

The Assam Movement

The agitation, which began from the Mangaldoi constituency in 1979 due to the sudden emergence of illegal Bangladeshis, reached its crescendo and spread like wildfire throughout the Brahmaputra valley. This incident triggered the start of the massive Assam Movement led by the All Assam Students' Union (AASU) and lasted for six years starting in 1979. This was, by far, the largest political movement predominantly led by college students. The Golap Borbora–led state government under the Janata Party was destabilized and President's Rule was imposed in Assam between December 1979 and December 1980. Due to a stiff opposition to the old electoral rolls, the Lok Sabha elections held in December 1979 were a complete failure. Out of fourteen Lok Sabha seats, elections couldn't be held in twelve seats and they went unfilled.

Later, when the assembly elections were held in 1980, Anwara Taimur was elected as the first woman chief minister of Assam. She held the office over 1980 and 1981. The choice of Taimur seems interesting in the wake of what had been happening on ground in Assam. Taimur, though an ethnic Assamese Muslim, was elected to the state assembly from a constituency heavily dominated by Bengali Muslim migrants.[4] She, therefore, primarily represented the Muslim immigrant interests. By installing a Muslim on the chief minister's seat in the thick of the huge storm, the Congress tried to send a clear signal to the Muslim vote bank it had nurtured and relied upon. It wanted to assert that despite all probable backlash, the political interests of the new migrants from Bangladesh would be guarded.[5] This move was a clear departure from the Congress's earlier position to persuade Assamese Muslim politicians not to aspire for the top post in the state. Instead 'they were encouraged to seek greener pastures in the pan-Indian arena, because it was feared that their chief ministership could be read as a sign of growing immigrant power'.[6] Anwara Taimur met her predictable political end soon after her anointment to the top post.

Political turbulence led to rising tensions and when lawlessness increased again, the President's Rule was reimposed in the state. When the reappointment of the chief minister took place, Taimur was replaced by Kesab Gogoi. By choosing an Assamese Muslim to guard its political positioning, the Congress had tested the waters of its newfound communal politics, and on seeing it fail, appointed Kesab Gogoi. However, he too fell to the political volatility within the state.

Despite shrewd political calculation and manipulation, the tension and emotions did not simmer down. Agitation continued in the state even after this reshuffle and perception reorganization. In fact, the divides between the clashing camps increased further. In such a situation, the Congress party, led by the then prime minister Indira Gandhi, should have read the writing on the wall and taken a tough stand with regard to updating the electoral rolls.

As is with every public movement, the Assam Movement also began with a great sense of optimism and festivity, marked by the non-violent nature of protests. The resistance was so organized that even the Assamese printing presses refused to print the old electoral rolls that had been used for the parliamentary elections of 1979.[7] Even the government paraphernalia openly supported the movement. The police avoided any confrontation with the agitators. The movement garnered support from diverse groups, such as the plain tribes, especially the Tiwas, Rabhas, Bodos and the tea plantation workers. Overall, an estimated 2 million people[8] courted arrest throughout the state in the initial phase of the movement.

The Nellie Massacre

Immigration into Assam wasn't just affecting the delicate ethnic balance but also the political. It was the latter that caused immediate and more dramatic reaction. This political unrest in the state would not have abated unless electoral rolls were revised. Considering the miraculously large new constituency that the Congress had allegedly built from across the border, it wished to continue nurturing this vote bank. The revision of rolls was clearly not a viable political option for them. On the other hand, the most important demand of the agitators led by the AASU was to seek a full revision of the electoral rolls before any elections were conducted in the state. The two camps came to an open confrontation in 1983 when the Indira Gandhi government at the Centre decided to conduct the state assembly elections without changing the electoral rolls. All hell broke loose in Assam

As part of standard operating procedure, the Election Commission seeks report from the Union home ministry on the preparedness of its security forces to conduct a free and fair election. Usually, it is very difficult for the Centre to accept that it cannot conduct the elections even with full security deployment as it sends a wrong signal on part of the nation's security establishment. The Khalistani Movement in Punjab, for instance, had undermined the authority and control of the central government. Partly to demonstrate that the government was firmly in control and partly to continue with the signature iron fist policy of Indira Gandhi, elections were thrust upon Assam. Despite warnings from intelligence reports and speculation by local police that the entire state of Assam would be flung into lawlessness if elections were forced upon the state, the central government at that time did not back down and went ahead with its decision to conduct the polls. By dishonouring the intelligence inputs the state was forced into a political turmoil.[9]

Between 7 January and 21 February in 1983—the day of the announcement of the polling till the end of polling—there were several incidents of violence across the state. The arson, bloodshed, looting and lawlessness reached its peak on 18 February 1983, when more than 1000 people were lynched in and around Nellie, a place just off the National Highway 27, around 70 km from Guwahati.

The Nellie massacre polarized the entire state on the issue of ethnic clashes and violence. Depending on the demographic assessment and geographical location, the Assamese–Bengali and/or Hindu–Muslim divide fomented and further stirred up sentiments. Divided neatly in camps and communities, the state followed the prophetic plot of the warning signs.

The elections recorded remarkably low voter turnout in areas dominated by ethnic Assamese. For instance, the Dhemaji constituency had 0.40 per cent and Dhakuakhana had 0.85 per cent turnout. Several other constituencies reported similar negligible turnout. The 1983 victory of the Congress party in the assembly elections, in hindsight, seems a win under very hostile circumstances. And it did fail the test of time.

Assam agitators were given a clear sign by then prime minister Indira Gandhi that if at all they wanted to talk to the central government and leadership in Delhi over their demands and grievances, they would have to route and mediate the discussion via the Hiteshwar Saikia–led state government. The writing on the wall was very clear. The agitators had to recognize the political validity of the Congress in order to negotiate their demands.

After two-year-long negotiations that went back and forth, the Assam Accord was signed in 1985 between the AASU and the Government of India in Delhi. According to the accord, those migrants who came to Assam after March 1971 would be deported. Those who came between January 1961 and March 1971 would be disenfranchised for the next ten years. It was further agreed that the government formed after the 1983 elections would resign and make way for fresh elections in the state based on new electoral rolls. Having won the battle of the mass agitation, some AASU leaders launched the AGP. This political party changed the political narrative and discourse of Assam for at least the next two decades.

The state witnessed a re-election in 1985, wherein the AGP trumped the Congress party, reducing the national party to a mere twenty-five seats. Prafulla Mahanta, at the age of thirty-two, became the chief minister, with a cabinet where the average age was less than forty. The AGP's ascendance to Dispur was marked by euphoria and wild public support.

The voice of democracy in Assam decisively dismissed the Congress's brand of communal politics. People held open their doors and kitchens for a cash-starved, young party during elections. Slogans were coined and popularized by the people themselves and the elections became a people's celebration of democracy rather than a party's battle.

After six long years of massive student's agitations led by the AASU, India's first truly young students' government had come to power in Assam with a 'right-wing' ideology at its core which was so politically unfashionable in that era of communist revolutions.

This sentiment is exactly what seemed to be mirrored in 2016. The people of Assam chose to fight the elections as if they held an active stake in the process and as if it was not the party's but their own campaign. The wave that swept Assam in 2016 was similar, and perhaps stronger, than the one that swept through Assam in 1985.

Disenchantment with the AGP

While the meteoric rise of the AGP was miraculous, its fall from glory was even more stunning. The patriots turned politicians who filled the ranks of the AGP-led government had serious charges of corruption and scandals levelled against them in its tenure from 1985 to 1990. The government also failed to implement the Assam Accord and deliver on its core promise of resolving the immigration crisis. The smack of arrogance that surrounded the young leaders alienated the mass support base. The fall of the AGP saw a simultaneous rise of the ULFA. The halo that had initially surrounded Prafulla Mahanta and his colleagues seemed to have been transferred the ULFA cadres, who made an emotional pledge to complete the unfinished agenda of the AGP. It made the case that political parties could not be trusted to protect Assam's interest. The new saviours of Assam were the gun-toting dreaded militants of the ULFA.

Both the AGP and the ULFA leaders were made of the same mould—both organizations were products of the Assam Movement and led by young lads motivated by similar issues of illegal migration, the stepbrotherly attitude of the Centre towards Assam and exploitation of its resources against the interest of the state. Seven youths, led by Arabinda Rajkhowa, Paresh Barua and Anup Chetia, founded the ULFA on 7 April 1979 at the precincts of Rang Ghar—a fifteenth-century iconic sports pavilion of the Ahom kingdom. The organization decided that it would strive to attain its targets through an armed struggle against the Indian state. The very first target of the ULFA was Hiteshwar Saikia, the then state home minister and the future chief minister of Assam, when a hand grenade was hurled at him in 1980. Saikia narrowly escaped the attack. This incident marked the beginning of the violent streak that would come to be associated with the ULFA. It continued to sporadically plan political killings and lootings to reinforce its presence in the region. The armed rebellion intensified after Delhi imposed elections in 1983. By 1985, the ULFA had become a household name with massive following among the youth. Bhupen Hazarika, in one of his songs embodied the popular feeling about the organization in those times. The lyrics of the song are: 'I salute mother Assam and I dress up to go to war. I salute the river Luit [another name for the Brahmaputra river] and offer puja to Goddess Kamakhya; with your blessings and oath, I am off to war.'[10] What happened over the next decade was a long phase of unending violence.

The hobnobbing of the ULFA and the AGP leaders was a well-established fact. The AGP was perceived as an over-the-ground political arm of the ULFA. However, post 1985, when the AGP came to power, the relationship became more complex. Paresh Barua, the commander-in-chief of the ULFA, lamented in a cryptic tone '[W]ith the stroke of chance they [AGP cadres] became ministers and we came to jungles'.[11]

Early on, the ULFA had received substantial support from the state machinery of the AGP government. In fact, the state government provided easy support in the form of money and material that corrupted the minds of the ULFA leaders. A money-centric and arms-centric culture governed the organization and took the state support for granted. In a sustained fashion, a popular armed struggle deteriorated into terrorism. The mindless violence and overtures towards cross-border terror organizations depleted the ULFA's popular support.

The reign of terror unleashed by the ULFA cost the AGP dearly. The ULFA almost ran a parallel government and there was little semblance of any rule of law. While the AGP could buy some time from the Centre as it was part of the coalition government led by V.P. Singh, it could not last long. With the change of guard at the Centre and the appointment of Chandra Shekhar as the prime minister, Delhi cracked down heavily on ULFA's insurgency. President's Rule was imposed in Assam on 27 November 1990. On the same day, ULFA was declared an unlawful organization. For the next six months, the Indian Army executed its anti-insurgency campaign code named Operation Bajrang against the ULFA. The army dismantled the organization's major training camps and arrested several of its prominent cadres. In a short period, the security forces had limited success in controlling the insurgency. Soon after, with changes in the political arena at the Centre, political parties in Assam swung back into the election mood.

The Hiteshwar Saikia Era

Hiteswar Saikia was the chief minister of Assam for two terms, first from February 1983 till December 1985 and then from June 1991 for a full five-year term till April 1996. A professor of history, Saikia's political maturity and organizing ability was unparalleled. His skills eventually caught the eye of Indira Gandhi, who reposed faith in him. In the midst of the constitutional crisis that appeared on Assam's political horizon post the 1983 elections, Saikia was made the chief minister. He had a proven record of steering the Congress through the toughest of times and also being at the helm during the highly emotive student movement. He was principally responsible for bringing AASU leaders to the negotiating table and the signing of the Assam Accord. Impressed by his handling of the delicate ethnonationalist situation in Assam, Rajiv Gandhi had also entrusted upon him the responsibility of solving the Mizo insurgency problem. The Mizo crisis was similar to the Assam problem in its tone and tenor. Post the 1985 elections, Saikia was sent to Mizoram as its Lt Governor. His key goals were set out—bringing normalcy back to the hill state and bringing the insurgent groups in to sign the Mizo Accord, in line with Assam Accord, with the central government. After successfully delivering on the objectives set out for him in Mizoram, Saikia was back at the helm of Assam Congress to prepare the party for the 1991 state elections.

Behind the stupendous political successes of Saikia lie his skilled manoeuvring, which almost always outsmarted his opponents. While the Saikia government was competing for legitimacy with the AASU-led Assam Movement, Saikia himself tried to create a rift in the broad base support of the movement. His machinations created a sense of doubt among the Muslim members of the AASU that the movement had taken a 'pro-Hindu communal tilt'.[12] The Muslim leaders demanded that the AASU provide a clearer definition of 'foreigner' in its anti-migrant fight. A similar sense of insecurity was instilled in the minds of other ethnic minorities like the Bodos, tea garden workers and Nepalis. The Saikia government was successful in creating a perception that the Assam Movement was led by and for the upper-caste Hindu Assamese. As a result, the fault lines were exposed in the Assamese national formation. The AASU leaders had to repeatedly call for political unity to sustain the momentum of the movement. The growing internal rifts in the organization served as a prime reason for drawing the AASU leadership to the negotiating table with the government.

During the AGP regime, Saikia orchestrated yet another incident. Bharat Narah, a prominent student leader of Assam Movement, was made the forest minister in the AGP government. Saikia introduced him to Jahanara Chaudhary, a Muslim woman from Guwahati's Gandhi Basti, who later renamed herself Ranee Narah. The two got married in 1986. According to a few analysts, this supposedly honey-trapped marriage was Hiteshwar Saikia's coup against the first right-wing government of the state.[13] While on the surface this was a marriage of two lovers, deep within it carried huge symbolic value. Marriages such as these were seen as a systematic infiltration of the migrants in the Assamese community. Saikia did achieve his target of breaking the AGP as the Narah couple eventually joined the Congress party and have remained loyal soldiers of the Nehru–Gandhi political dynasty for over twenty-five years.

Saikia was again entrusted the responsibility of leading the Congress's campaign in 1991. He began his meticulous planning combined with rigorous campaigning. The Congress's campaign was emboldened by the fact that the ULFA decided not to support the AGP covertly or overtly. Saikia focused on bringing back the traditional vote bank of the Congress into the party's fold. This included Bengali-speaking voters and the tea garden workers. Several plains tribes, especially the Bodos, were thoroughly disgruntled by the AGP and came back to the Congress.

Assam's ethnopolitical reality made it difficult for the AGP to politically survive only on the vote bank of ethnic Assamese. They had to reach out to other ethnic minorities to build a rainbow coalition of sorts. To understand these political compulsions, one needs to understand a small but highly important political formation in the 1985 elections called United Minorities Front (UMF). The UMF was predominantly constituted of ex-Congress leaders of Bengali descent—both Hindu and Muslim Bengalis. While for the AGP the main existential issue was the Assam Accord, the UMF's sole demand was to scrap the Accord. In the 1985 elections, where the AGP won sixty-four seats with a 32.5 per cent vote share in its wave election, the UMF managed to secure seventeen seats. Realizing the demographic reality, AGP's main campaign slogan for 1991 elections was 'Minorities are not Foreigners, AGP for all, all for AGP'—a clever yet practical coinage of words.

Eventually, in June 1991, the Congress won the required majority of seats in the state assembly, securing a slender vote share of 28 per cent. With Hiteshwar Saikia back at the helm, he once again skilfully began negotiating with the ULFA. He succeeded in splitting the ULFA cadres into two groups—one favouring the suspension of operations and dialogue, and the other opposing it. Saikia employed a carrot and stick policy in dealing with the ULFA, which did yield some results. Several cadres surrendered and many others were arrested. However, in September 1991, Saikia recommended a second round of military operations to control the insurgency after the ULFA kidnapped fifteen senior government officials. This operation was code named Operation Rhino. The military crackdown virtually eliminated the middle leadership of the ULFA. Thousands of cadres were arrested. The brutality of the operation vastly curtailed insurgency in Assam.

The perverse incentives offered by the Saikia government to the Surrendered ULFA cadres created a new wave of violence that gripped the state. These ex-militants were allowed to keep weapons for self-protection and were additionally given government security cover. Later these Surrendered ULFA cadres, known as the SULFA, became part of the state machinery whose services were often utilized to eliminate ULFA cadres.

Saikia's dream of a negotiated settlement of the ULFA-led insurgency problem remained unfulfilled. He died on 22 April 1996 in the midst of the next round of state elections. The AGP's electoral plank in the run-up to the 1996 assembly elections was the withdrawal of the army from Assam. The AGP gained significant popularity due to its firm stand of curtailing the atrocities committed by the security establishment. The ULFA went on a massive offensive during the 1996 elections. It kidnapped and killed family members of political parties, especially those of Congress party members. 'The deal was that the ULFA would create a reign of terror which would facilitate the return of AGP.'[14] This bonhomie was soon to change.

The 1996 elections were won by the AGP and Prafulla Kumar Mahanta was reinstated as the chief minister of Assam. The second AGP regime was marred by total political chaos and violence right from the beginning. AGP's relationship with the ULFA deteriorated soon after the elections. Mahanta realized that 'if the ULFA continues its reign of terror, he would not survive politically, and therefore he decided to crackdown on ULFA before it was too late'.[15] A Unified Command Structure was put in place to coordinate the efforts of army, state police and paramilitary forces in anti-insurgency operations. The Congress has time and again accused[16] the AGP-led government of using SULFA cadres to kill the friends, family and sympathizers of ULFA insurgents.[17] The extrajudicial killings by 'unknown assailants' were infamously referred to as 'secret killings'. These killings dominated the discourse of the AGP government till the end of its term in 2001.

The Tarun Gogoi Era

A chief minister who ruled Assam for three consecutive terms between 2001 and 2016, Tarun Gogoi is a name that occupies a dignified space in the history of Assam politics. The rhetoric of electoral acrimony aside, he has been one of the most astute politicians in the Congress camp. He is one of the few politicians of Assam who has made it big not just at the state level but also at the Centre.

As an Indira Gandhi and Rajiv Gandhi loyalist, Gogoi has held several crucial organizational roles in the Congress party, serving as the joint secretary of the AICC twice and also as the general secretary once. He served as the Union cabinet minister later and was also a part of many central government committees. Gogoi's political career in the state started off as a member of the Municipal Board in Jorhat. He was elected to the fifth Lok Sabha as an MP and continued his political journey as an MP for six terms. He also served the state as an MLA for four terms.

Gogoi's ascendance to power in Assam bypassing Hiteshwar Saikia and Bhumidhar Barman is a story about blunt, calculative and populist politics that reflects a lot about Gogoi's style of politics. Despite Gogoi's love for luxury and his self-avowed fondness for opulent living, he has held on to the roots of Assam's rural and agrarian culture. The Tai-Ahom community that he belongs to and his deep involvement with Upper Assam as an MP and later as an MLA made Gogoi's hold over Upper Assam's politics a difficult one to ignore.

During the 2011 assembly elections, Gogoi projected his Ahom identity as a justification to rule over Assam, and by raising the question 'Who is Badruddin Ajmal' drove home the identity question. His constant invocations of his Ahom identity and reference to Lachit's blood coursing through his veins have made a case for Gogoi receiving popular support from the people of Assam.

Gogoi's practical and pragmatic approach to politics was well received within the Congress party and amidst the public as well until he lost the battle against his own identity conflict as a politician and a father. His support for his son Gaurav Gogoi in granting him representation in Kaliabor constituency, closer to his turf in Titabor and one which Tarun Gogoi represented throughout his political career, went beyond a politician's role and entered the realm of a father's role who was looking for a political heir.

Local leaders of Assam—some who had spent their entire lives honing their constituencies and building the party—did not take to an 'imported', metropolitan and seemingly less interested Gaurav. Himanta Biswa Sarma openly rebelled as a result of this. It is opined that Tarun Gogoi, who has been an exemplum of a leader, allowed his fatherly instincts to get the better of him and resulted in the decline of a lifelong political capital.

However, Gogoi must be credited for the political handling of the Assam situation. The legacy of a lawless state, thanks to the effects of anti-state activities in Assam, diminished, and the condition stabilized properly only under Gogoi's reign. Like it happens for most popular leaders, Gogoi's first two terms were marked by developmental achievements that a state could be proud of, but the decline in his politics in the later part of his chief ministerial career resulted in Assam slipping from the Congress's hands.

The 2016 elections, for instance, saw a side of Tarun Gogoi that was weary and aged and not up to the political astuteness he had stood for. Not only did he commit major mistakes in posturing himself and the party, he chose to ignore the writing on the wall quite blatantly. Despite knowing that he should have stepped down from the chief minister's post to pave the way for the next rung of leadership, he chose to stay a little longer until his son Gaurav could take over from him. In his doggedness to promote Gaurav, he lost Himanta.

Similarly, Gogoi chose to ignore the numerical logic and not ally with the regional players. He also failed to weave a narrative like he did earlier to retain Assam for himself and the Congress.

Who is Badruddin Ajmal?

Badruddin Ajmal does not like people judging him by his skullcap or his ankle-high pyjama and kurta. This cleric-cum-business-tycoon-cum-politician, who founded the All-India United Democratic Front (AIUDF), will settle for nothing less than the secular tag for his party. A scholar from Deoband in Uttar Pradesh, his family owns most of Hojai town, in the Nagaon district in Assam. His family also owns the largest agar plantation near Hojai, Asia's largest rural charitable hospital—the 500-bed Haji Abdul Majid Memorial Hospital and Research Centre—and Asia's richest NGO, Markaj-ul Maaris and, of course, one of the world's biggest perfume businesses. He is a person respected for his generous nature and his healing power.

That such a man can easily match the financial powers of mainstream political parties is beyond doubt. But in the case of Badruddin Ajmal, he has also been helped by the changing demographic character of Assam. While Muslims constituted 30.9 per cent of the population in 2001, this share jumped to

34.2 per cent in 2011. In 2001, only six districts had a Muslim majority. In 2011, Muslims constituted the majority in nine districts.

Interestingly, the working president of his party, Aditya Langthsa, belongs to the Dimasa tribe. He claims that the AIUDF should not be seen as a Muslim party just because it was founded by a Muslim cleric. In the words of Ajmal, 'Our party's policy is clear—we are Axomiya (Assamese), we had been Axomiya, and we will die as Axomiya.' Badruddin himself draws a distinction between himself and Asaduddin Oiwasi, between the AIUDF and the Hyderabad-based All-India Majlis-e-Ittehadul Muslimeen, saying that his party has non-Muslim MLAs and his working president is a tribesman. Moreover, in the 2014 parliamentary elections, a prominent Hindu named Radheshyam Biswas won from the Karimgunj constituency on the AIUDF ticket. In the last Bodo Tribal Council elections, the AIUDF won four seats, although critics say that this became possible due to an increase in the Muslim population in the Bodo Tribal Council area.

There is, however, no doubt that the AIUDF has expanded its reach far and wide in Assam. In the 2009 Lok Sabha polls, its only success was in the Dhubri constituency, but in 2014 it bagged three Lok Sabha seats—Dhubri, Barpeta and Karimganj. In the 2006 assembly elections, the AIUDF won ten seats but in the assembly poll of 2011, the figure jumped to eighteen. Similarly, in the 2011 assembly polls, the AIUDF vote share was 12.6 per cent, increasing to 15 per cent in 2014. In the 2014 parliamentary elections, the AIUDF had established comfortable leads in twenty-four assembly constituencies.

Badruddin Ajmal tried to make a strong effort to position himself as a pan-Assamese leader. To achieve that he had to shed the image of being a Muslim leader. Using the largesse of his sprawling business empire, he donated Rs 60 lakh to a *satra* (monastery) that traces its origin to the Vaishnavite traditions. He also initiated an education programme called Ajmal National Rural Education Memorial to adopt thirteen unaided schools and thirteen colleges to help out both teachers and students financially, irrespective of their caste or religion. In spite of his positioning, the fact remains that in the electoral calculus the AIUDF's strength lies in being a Muslim party.

Outside of Kashmir, Muslims in Assam constitute, percentage-wise, the single-largest presence in any state. They account for 35 per cent of the state population. Numerically, they are second only to Muslims in Uttar Pradesh. Even the 2011 assembly elections had shown that sixteen of AIUDF's seats were spread across nine districts where Muslims, especially Bengali-speaking Muslims, were in majority. In the last election, the AIUDF won eighteen seats, a jump from the eight seats it won in the 2006 elections, when the party was just six months old.

The AIUDF was founded after the repeal of the Illegal Migrants (Determination by Tribunals) Act in 2005. With his flowing beard and a skullcap, Badruddin Ajmal, the AIUDF founder, has since been perceived by many in Assam as the protector of the interests of illegal Muslim immigrants from Bangladesh. In the 2014 Lok Sabha polls, Ajmal fielded his brother Sirajuddin from Kaliabor against the sitting MP and Gogoi's brother Dip Gogoi. In 2016, Sirajuddin was shifted to

Barpeta, while Gogoi's son Gaurav was the Congress candidate from Kaliabor in an alleged tactic understanding. 'It's crystal clear that Ajmal is helping Gogoi ensure a comfortable victory for Gaurav. The allegations of a secret pact first came to the fore when in February the AIUDF vice president Ataur Rahman Mazarbhuyan abstained from voting in the Rajya Sabha elections, and thereby ensured that all three candidates from the Congress and Bodoland People's Front won.'[18]

Jatiyo Nayak Sarbananda Sonowal

For the 2016 elections, Sarbananda Sonowal was chosen as the BJP's chief ministerial candidate by consensus. Sonowal was serving as the minister of state for youth affairs and sports when the announcement was made on 28 January 2015.

Hailed as the *Jatiyo Nayak* by the AASU in Assam over his role in scrapping the Illegal Migrants (Determination by Tribunals) Act, his tough stand against the illegal Bangladeshi immigrants during the course of his political career had propelled him to the position of a mass leader of universal appeal in Assam.

Sarbananda Sonowal joined the BJP in 2011. He rose from being the party president in 2014 to being granted a Lok Sabha ticket from Lakhimpur, then being a Union minister and finally being announced the party's chief ministerial candidate. His rise in the party ranks has been unprecedented.

Sarbananda Sonowal was an ex-AGP leader who joined the BJP in 2011. Unlike most of his contemporaries, Sarbananda did not have the baggage of corruption and enjoyed public goodwill. His affability added to him being the chosen one.

As a Union minister of youth affairs and sports, Sonowal had done all he could to support talent from the North-east and put the region on the national and global map. He hosted the XII South Asian Games (SAG) in Guwahati and Shillong after a series of delays and controversies. This was the first time a North-eastern state in the country had hosted an international sports event and popularized the culture of the state. Tikhor, the one-horned-rhino mascot, and *gamosa*, the traditional white-and-red cloth, the two prized repositories of the cultural heritage of Assam became the symbol of the SAG. Eight countries and 2762 athletes participated in more than 228 events across twenty-two sports. Sonowal ensured that the official song of the SAG was also a cultural tribute to Assam. He chose Bhupen Hazarika's 'Ei Prithibi Ek Krirangan' as the games anthem.

All these contributions coupled with Sonowal's image, gave a facelift to the BJP. A young and dynamic Union minister from Assam against an ageing Tarun Gogoi was a contrast that was designed to drive home an obvious choice in the minds of the voters.

Machiavelli of the North-east: Himanta Biswa Sarma

Himanta Biswa Sarma is one of the most politically savvy and erudite leaders in not just Assam but also in the entire North-east. While still in his late forties, Sarma has had an illustrious political career spanning over three decades. He has worked with the who's who of Assamese politics right from the days of the AASU, the AGP to being a loyal Congress party worker for the past twenty years. Sarma is a product of the subnational Assam Movement of the 1980s that sought to protect the rights of indigenous peoples against those of foreigners or migrants. The young Sarma began his political activism right from his school days when he was a key courier boy relaying secret messages among the top rung of the AASU leaders. He built on his student politics and later served as the general secretary of Cotton College in Guwahati from 1991 to 1992.

Sarma considers himself a mentee of the Congress politician, Hiteshwar Saikia. He speaks with fondness and great respect of how Saikia not just taught him the rules of this game, but also backed him up every time he needed support. He recounts how he first met Hiteshwar Saikia in the early 1990s while Sarma was a student leader at the Cotton College. Saikia developed a deep fondness for Sarma during this meeting. Soon after, Saikia invited Sarma on the latter's birthday and surprisingly made him the chairman of the state youth welfare committee. Ever since then, the chairman post of Youth Welfare Committee has been touted as the most prestigious post for a promising young politician.

Sarma's journey in the Congress progressed from him collecting newspaper clippings of the day to be sent to Saikia every morning to being Saikia's blue-eyed boy. His closeness to Saikia and his political ambitions earned him several political rivals early on in his career. Saikia's death in 1996 came as a big jolt for him. He was left without a political godfather who could have firmly anchored his political debut, and he lost his first electoral battle in 1996 from Jalukbari. His legal expertise served him well during his politically sterile years. He gave free legal counsel in his constituency to those in need of legal aid. He took to the streets against cases of secret killings during the AGP regime. Finally, his patience paid off. He defeated one of AGP's most prominent leaders, Bhrigu Kumar Phukan, from

Jalukabari constituency in the 2001 state elections, which saw a huge anti-incumbency wave against the AGP government. Sarma rapidly marched forward on his political journey. He was made planning and development minister in 2002 and a cabinet minister in 2006 holding critical portfolios under the Tarun Gogoi regimes.

By 2011, Sarma had evolved into one of the most towering Congress leaders of Assam. He was troubleshooter-in-chief for the state government and state Congress unit. The 2011 election campaign was primarily designed and meticulously planned by him. Under the leadership of Tarun Gogoi and the strategic planning of Sarma, the Congress won the 2011 elections with a thumping majority. The party alone won seventy-eight out of 126 assembly seats—an unprecedented seat share in the recent political history of Assam.

By this time Sarma's political invincibility had fuelled his ambitions even more. He started harbouring aims for the top post in the state. The then Congress general secretary and party in-charge of Assam, Digvijay Singh, pushed his name for the chief ministerial post instead of the incumbent Gogoi. At the same time, Gogoi rushed to Delhi to re-convince party president Sonia Gandhi of his leadership. Sarma had to reluctantly back down, though his intense ambition could not be thwarted.

Over time, the organizational fractures deepened in the state Congress unit. The situation reached an inflection point when Tarun Gogoi decided to politically promote his son Gaurav Gogoi. Gradually, the junior Gogoi started calling the shots in the party much to the dismay and resentment of party veterans, especially Sarma.

Around 2014, when the United Progressive Alliance government at the Centre was battered by serious corruption charges and was faced by a political challenge from Narendra Modi, Sarma began a rebellion in Assam. Sarma asserted that Tarun Gogoi no longer enjoyed the support of Congress MLAs and more than fifty-five of them were demanding a change of guard in Assam. The matter took an ugly turn and was soon escalated to the Congress's central leadership.

In a meeting called by Rahul Gandhi, which included the then chief minister of Assam, Tarun Gogoi, Assam Pradesh Congress Committee chief, Anjan Dutta, party general secretary in-charge of Assam, C.P. Joshi, and Sarma, regarding the political affairs of the party in the state, Joshi and Gogoi had broken into a fist-thumping feud.[19] Unaffected by the fight and refusing to rise up to the occasion as a leader, Rahul Gandhi paid little heed to the conversation. Instead, he started playing with his pet dog and continued to do so despite the fight between the two senior-most leaders of the party reaching a bitter level. Meanwhile, the dog started to nibble on the biscuits meant for the guests in the room. Rahul still did not bother to intervene and neither did he feel it necessary to replace the plate of biscuits![20,21]

On another occasion, in yet another meeting to discuss the situation in Assam, Rahul asked Himanta Biswa Sarma to keep the discussion limited to a mere two-minute exercise. An elaborate presentation prepared by a veteran leader of the party regarding the prospects of the state and the political situation within the party was cut short by the Congress vice president and asked to be wrapped up within the stipulated two minutes. For any committed worker of the party, and that too a senior, impressive and popular leader as Sarma, it would have been too much of an insult to travel so far, receive such a treatment and be asked to submit to the whims of Rahul Gandhi.

The fruitless meeting with central Congress leaders left Himanta Biswa Sarma with little hope. Ironically, Digvijay Singh, the former in-charge of Assam Pradesh Congress Committee, advised Sarma to leave the Congress and join the BJP.[22] It was then that Sarma opened back channel discussions with Ram Madhav, a veteran RSS *pracharak* who was also managing the 2014 election campaign. The machinations of Sarma ensured that the Congress was defeated in the 2014 Lok Sabha elections. The party won only three seats from the state out of a total of fourteen seats. Over the next year or so, Sarma continued his negotiations with Ram Madhav for joining the BJP. The discussions concluded in August 2015, when Sarma formally joined the BJP at Amit Shah's official residence in Delhi. Sarma claimed to have the support of fifty-five Congress MLAs who were ready to follow him. Out of these, the BJP picked nine MLAs who, along with Sarma, joined the party.

Relaunching a political career is fraught with risks. Especially when several rank and file members of the new party are opposed to the person's entry. The party's cadres were reluctant to admit Sarma also because he had been very vocal against the BJP ideology until only a few days before joining them. Sarbananda Sonowal was also uncomfortable with the induction of Sarma, knowing his ambitions well. However, Sarma being a realist, quickly smoothed over the issues and built a working rapport with Sonowal.

Once touted as the right hand of Tarun Gogoi, Sarma's entry and subsequent rise in the BJP was even more spectacular. He is known for basing his strategic moves on his ability to read the people's pulse. Despite the various corruption charges levelled against Sarma at different points in time during his political career, he enjoys the goodwill of the public, the party men and whoever works with him.

chapter three

FIVE DECADES OF THE SANGH

मयि सर्वाणि कर्माणि संन्यस्याध्यात्मचेतसा।
निराशीर्निर्ममो भूत्वा युध्यस्व विगतज्वरः।।3.30।।

('Therefore, O Arjuna, surrendering all your works unto Me, with mind intent on Me, and without desire for gain and free from egoism and lethargy, fight.')

—Shrimad Bhagwat Gita

~

There is a tradition of singing a specific type of folk song called *jhoomar* during celebratory pre-wedding rituals in Bihar. Among the many types of jhoomars are songs that narrate mythological stories. These folk songs are generally passed on orally by women from one generation to the other. These jhoomars are a repository of the rich cultural handover. One of the authors' grandmothers in Bihar narrated the story of Aniruddha, a prince from present-day Gujarat, and Usha, a princess from present-day Assam, in one of the traditional jhoomars with great gusto.

The story goes that Banasura, the king of Sonitpur (present-day Tezpur in Assam) and a Shiva devotee, had a very beautiful daughter, Usha. Usha saw a young man in her dream one day and fell in love with him. One of her friends, Chitralekha, the daughter of Kumbhanda, a minister in Banasura's kingdom, was a talented artist with supernatural powers. Upon hearing the dream, Chitralekha drew the face of the young man.

The picture drawn by Chitralekha was identified as that of Aniruddha, the grandson of Dwarikadhish, Lord Krishna. Chitralekha brought Aniruddha from Dwarka (in Gujarat) to Usha in Sonitpur. Aniruddha also fell in love with Usha, and they wanted to get married.

On learning of the situation, Banasura was very angry. Meanwhile, when Krishna heard that his grandson had been abducted and was in Sonitpur, he set out to rescue Aniruddha along with his elder brother, Balarama and his son, Pradyumna.

A great battle was fought. Banasura staged a fierce counter-attack against Krishna. Lord Shiva also joined the battle against Krishna in order to protect Banasura. Upon sensing Banasura's imminent defeat, Shiva implored Krishna to not kill his devotee. Krishna agreed to this request.

Later Banasura not just prostrated before Krishna but also joined in the wedding celebration of Aniruddha and Usha. The lovers united to live happily ever after.

A journalist from Assam also recounted a similar tale to me during one of our conversations after the Assam elections. This striking similarity to the story sung as a jhoomar in Bihar by an illiterate lady, who has rarely travelled beyond her state, can barely read scriptures and histories and is most certainly not an agent of the larger state apparatus to appropriate Assam, denotes the idea of oneness within the Indian cultural civilization and reveals the cultural nationalism of our Bharatvarsha. This is the essence that Srimanta Sankardeva, one of the biggest cultural stalwarts of Assam, captures in his conceptualization of Bharatvarsha.

Bharatvarsha binds different and disparate cultures and societies together and nourishes the idea of oneness within the Indian cultural civilization. This is also the ideological fulcrum on which anti-India, pro-subnational political positions in Assam, such as the ULFA's ideology were negated and negotiated by the RSS, resulting in a fierce ideological battle for decades.

In the monolithic narrative that dominated Assam's contemporary politics, no one saw nationalism as a politically viable alternative or a rallying political thought. How did an organization like the RSS make a foray into a battered Assam in the late 1940s? What helped the Sangh, an organization that did not have roots in Assam, gain a firm foothold in the multilingual, multi-ethnic and multipolar state? How did the organization make such an indelible imprint in Assam that while interpreting the assembly election results in 2016, analysts[1] were forced to acknowledge its pervasive influence in galvanizing the support of the electorate?

The Beginnings of the RSS

The Muslim League's call to Direct Action in 1946 resulted in acute Hindu–Muslim polarization in East Bengal. Killings in Kolkata and riots in Noakhali were the direct result of this and caused the mass exodus of minority Hindus from Muslim-dominated areas in East Bengal. The exodus further intensified closer to the Partition in August 1947. On the eastern and western borders of India, land, people and property were fast changing to new names and identities. The mindless murders, rapes, abductions and other forms of violence dominated the Partition narrative of Punjab.

However, similar echoes of violence in the bordering areas of Assam rarely find reverberation in the Partition narrative. Mass exodus of Bengali Hindus and Muslims has continued to take place in the naturally porous borders between present-day Bangladesh and India, and resulted in a history of heart-rending violations of human rights over the years. The RSS started its first *seva* (service) in Assam in 1946 to help the ailing men and women suffering the brutalities of the riots and violence.

Dr Keshav Baliram Hedgewar founded the RSS on 27 September 1925 in Nagpur. Almost two decades later, on 28 October 1946, the Sangh held its first *shakha* in Guwahati. Taking note of the request by a Marwari businessman, Keshav Dev Bawri, the Sangh sent three experienced pracharaks— Dadarao Parmarth, Vasant Rao Oak and Shri Krishna Paranjpe—to begin setting up of an arm of the RSS in Assam. Dada Rao Parmarth shifted to Shillong as the *prant* pracharak—an RSS ideologue who heads the activities of the region concerned. Shri Krishna Paranjpe went to Dibrugarh and Vasant Rao Oak settled down in Guwahati.

However, after Mahatma Gandhi's assassination in 1948, the RSS was banned. Participating in the nationwide satyagraha against the ban, Assam saw fifty-two activists protesting. Almost forty-six pracharaks in Assam were jailed. Dadarao Parmarth was taken ill and he returned to Nagpur.

In 1949, after the ban was lifted, Dattopant Thengdi succeeded Dadarao Parmarth and worked closely with Manohar Rao Harekar, a prant pracharak from Bengal. The same year, the first shakha was set up after the ban was organized. In November 1949, Guruji Madhav Sadashiv Golwalkar sent Thakur Ram Singh, a pracharak from Punjab, who was appointed the prant pracharak of Assam. During that time, Eknath Ranade was the *kshetriya* pracharak of Bengal, Assam and Orissa.[2]

Thakur Ram Singh hailed from Himachal Pradesh and had worked in Punjab during the peak of Partition. He initiated the Akhil Bharatiya Itihas Sankalan Yojana, a subsidiary organization of the RSS, which was formally founded in 1978–79 with the objective of writing history from an anti-British, nationalist perspective.

In 1950, Assam was facing the effects of an earthquake. Guruji Golwalkar visited the affected areas and started an organization named Bhukamp Peedit Sahayata Samiti. This was accepted and appreciated quite well in Assam. As a far-fetched idea shared by pracharaks active in Assam for more than five decades, the Sangh's first foray into the public space as offering seva was received with much admiration.[3]

The Ideologies at Play in Assam

In the imagination of the RSS, Assam was a wounded limb of the Indian civilization. The backdrop of Partition is an exegesis of the Sangh's conception in Assam. As the state's history had been punctuated by several violent movements, demands of nationalities within nationality and a narrative perennially vexed with the issue of cultural erosion, it provided the RSS ample reason to propagate the idea of integration on national issues.

In Assam, the Sangh saw an opportunity to fix the battered limb of a wounded Bharat Mata. The journey of the Sangh in

Assam also reflects the internal journey RSS embarked on to react and respond to a culturally diverse sociopolitical reality.

It is interesting to examine why the Assamese civilization with such deep roots in history and such strong sociocultural connections with the rest of India embarked on a visceral quest of identity and armed nationalism. It is equally compelling to observe how proponents of clashing streams of ideologies within this quest battled among themselves to prove the veracity of their narratives. While one tried to carve a new identity for Assam, the other tried to integrate the state with the larger nationhood.

The militant nationalism propagated by the ULFA can best be summed up in ULFA chairman, Arabinda Rajkhowa's words, 'Asom and Asom's identity is not part of India and Indian identity.'[4] In a similar vein, Ajit Bhuyan, one of the ideologues of ULFA writes, 'We in Assam often wonder as to why there has been so much concern to depict India as one nation state . . . The undisputable truth is "India is a multinational state, a land of innumerable nationalities, big or small, dominant or weak".'[5] Later, Parag Das, the torchbearer of ULFA ideology in one of his books avers, 'We are not getting carried away by an emotional branding of Bharat Mata and hence propagate one unified India.'[6]

While the passionate appeal of ULFA found resonance among its cadre, there was an equally potent voice of protest dismissing the grander designs of ULFA. Prof. Udayon Misra, responding to the ULFA chairman, says, 'In trying to build up his argument, the ULFA Chairman has made a selective reading of Assam's recent history . . . He has not mentioned the participation of the Assamese masses in the freedom struggle against the British and the role played by the countless leading intellectuals in the Congress-led movement. Not to speak of reformer saints like Sankardeva for whom "Bharatvarsha" was such an important concept and who contributed immensely to bringing Assam within the Indian "mainstream".[7]

The limits of ULFA lay in its stubborn appropriation of colonial and postcolonial history of Assam from the lens of anti-Delhi-ism and subnationalism. Noted academician and author, Prof. Nani Gopal Mahanta traces the failure of the ULFA in the following words, 'Terror-driven agenda with exclusive focus on arms, international network, money and a hopeless ideology have gradually made ULFA a near irrelevant force in Assam . . . Parag's greatest failure was that he failed to understand the pulse of the people with whom he wanted to liberate Assam from India.'[8]

Against this strong and militant ideological force of the ULFA, the Sangh remained committed to its cherished goal of a unified Bharat Mata. The rootedness of the Sangh in celebrating the historical and cultural DNA of Assam and its people and in recounting the ancient connection of Assam with the rest of India was a steep departure from the ULFA brand of nationalism.

The RSS traced the history of Assam way back in time and recreated the ancient glories of Pragjyotishpur and Kamrupa (AD 4th century). The reference to these kingdoms has been made in quasi-mythical-historical texts like Ramayana, Mahabharata and *Kalikha Purana*, and travelled from Assam to the rest of the Indian society. In bringing these to the fore, the Sangh created a sense of pride in the Assamese people.

For example, during local festivities like Bihu and Durga Puja, the swayamsevaks of the Sangh began erecting pandals to honour the portrait of Bharat Mata. With the vexed question of identity looming large in Assam, the RSS stitched the delicate narratives of regionalism and nationalism together by merging the national with the local through the invocation of an emotional idea of the motherland by introducing an element of belief and emotional appeal. The Sangh changed the ideological fulcrum of the debate in Assam and emerged as a credible alternative to the left or left-inspired portrayals of Assam. It took a long struggle to fructify and popularize the nationalist sentiment in Assam, which is often articulated by the Akhil Bharatiya Vidyarthi Parishad as '*Kachh ho ya Guwahati, apna desh apni maati* [Whether Kutch or Guwahati, it is one nation—our nation, our soil].'

By 1975, all districts in Assam had Sangh shakhas. The gradual brick-by-brick establishment of the Sangh in Assam has been a result of decades of perseverant work and selfless service by swayamsevaks from all across the country. Often the swayamsevaks and pracharaks were not from Assam. It took decades of commitment to prepare the local swayamsevaks for top organizational roles. Eventually, in 2014, RSS appointed a local Assamese, Baisistha Bujarbaruah, as the prant pracharak of Assam.

Most of the early swayamsevaks in Assam lived their entire lives in a culture and society so unique and different from theirs that they happily learnt to enjoy local cuisines, learnt local languages, adopted and adapted to local customs and traditions so that they could serve well the local population.

But this journey of the Sangh in Assam has not just been a romantic story lived by the Sangh in ideal conditions. Creating a counter narrative in an atmosphere of vitiated political and intellectual environment has been one of the greatest achievements of the Sangh. Even after losing so many swayamsevaks and pracharaks to violence, the RSS kept its firm resolve and commitment to achieve the goals of national integration.

Shukleshwar Medhi was an RSS pracharak who worked during the height of the ULFA agitation. Medhi's elder brother and another pracharak, Murli Manohar, were kidnapped and taken away by the ULFA in the late 1990s. The former returned but the latter never did. On 30 August 2005, Naba Hiranya, an ULFA militant killed Shukleshwar Medhi. Another pracharak, Pramod Dixit, was killed in Barpeta a couple of months later.

What has been the motivation and inspiration for these swayamsevaks from Kerala, Tamil Nadu, Punjab, Himachal Pradesh and other geographically and linguistically diverse pockets of the country to work in one of the most neglected areas of the country for some abstract goal of national integration, risking their lives, their families' well-being and putting all their personal assets to risk? This feeling of oneness with the entire country, this sense of sacrifice for the motherland and to serve her in the interior most pockets, this fearlessness to settle down at places which might be very diverse and different from the cultures they inhabit is the feeling that has failed the imagination of most intellectuals in the country. Nothing but either genuine or crafted neglect explains the absolute quietude in academic, social service and intellectual circles in acknowledging the selfless service of swayamsevaks, battling all kinds of violence and hardships in areas as remote as these. It is difficult to explain why this huge institution is bypassed in a disparaging tone and not critiqued in a comprehensive light.

It is also interesting to observe that though media and certain sections of the intellectual coterie keeps flinging controversies on to the RSS, there has been no sincere and honest attempt to understand the organization. Especially with respect to areas in the information dark-zones of the North-east like Assam, its gradual national integration is a story left widely unattended to and unheard of.

We are tempted to believe that this surge of a new kind of politics in states like Assam is an extension of the 'saffron surge', as labellers love to call it. They confuse the phenomenon of the gradual rootedness of the Sangh with the electoral wins in the rest of the country. But this hasty write-off of a nationalist ideology against the anti-Indian, subnational, subversive idea of Assamese identity is a disservice to the unique and undocumented historical phenomenon of decades of physical, ideological and political struggle on ground. These were the struggles that were challenging, co-opting and moulding the regional into the national in more ways than one.

The Assam Movement and the Remoulding of the RSS

The RSS was largely seen as a Krishna Bhakti Movement in Assam for a very long time. The local people could not see beyond the bhakti parampara (devotional activities) propagated by the RSS. As an extended arm of Sankardeva's tradition, teachings and bhakti, the organization remained a spiritual–cultural force to reckon with for very long. In the beginning, it was neither a potent ideological force in Assam nor did it manifest itself in any political inclinations and interests. However, the sociopolitical–

cultural contours of time that opened up in Assam and the nation at large during the late 1970s–80s prised open an opportunity for the RSS to assert its ideological commitments.

The 1970s were dotted by a series of incidents, making this a troubled phase for India. The idea of a united Indian nation state or Akhand Bharat (as the RSS calls it), had come under direct threat from separatist movements simultaneously active across most parts the country. The Jammu and Kashmir Liberation Front, the Khalistan National Council, the ULFA in the North-east and many other insurgent groups in the region challenged the authority of the Indian state. After the repeal of the Emergency in 1977, the Janata Party government came to power at the Centre.

Apart from regional and often subnational sentiments that had gained prominence in different parts of the country around the 1970s and 1980s, there was an impulsive hunger for nationalistic sentiment that could bind the country together. The monolithic mould of the Indian polity was creaking to give way to something new. It had created an antithesis for an alternative ideology—other than that represented by the status quo—to emerge.

This ideological national void was filled by the Ram Janmbhoomi Movement—spearheaded by the BJP—that rallied people across the geographical expanse of the country. The popularity of the Movement and the large-scale public participation in the Shila Poojan across the length and breadth of the nation, in the later 1980s and early 1990s, suggest the on-ground support and emotional reckoning for the dream of an India based on nationalistic ideals and principles. Though Assam did not emerge as the frontrunner of the Movement, the regional nationalist sentiments found solace in the core cultural protectionist agenda of Hindutva.

Post-Independence, the Assam Movement has been one of most significant, people-led movements in India. The movement did not just mean the emergence of a student body organization in the AASU, it also nurtured and harboured the future leaders of Assam—Prafulla Mahanta, Sarbananda Sonowal, Himanta Biswa Sarma—in its womb. The movement also meant the integration of Assam's primal concern for an individualized, unique and proud assertion of its culture with the resurgent cultural nationalism.

It was the time when the anti-foreigner movement was at its peak in Assam and under the commitment to Hindutva, the RSS found a way to assert itself beyond the sociocultural activities it had engaged in. With an open political articulation for and against the *bahiragat* (referring to those who have come from outside to Assam) community in Assam, the RSS was able to subtly but forcefully assert an ideological position cloaked in the rhetoric of cultural nationalism. In the light of these developments, it is interesting to note how the RSS emerged in the wake of the Assam Movement.

After the formation and consolidation of the AASU, in the wake of the Mangaldoi situation, in 1979, when the Assam Movement unfolded, the popular sentiment in Assam had gravitated from being indifferent or casual about migration from Bangladesh in Assam to taking a firm stand against the migrants in the state. Gauging the public sentiment and also extending its ideological support, the Sangh backed the mass movement. Besides, the AASU articulated a very strong sentiment about preserving and conserving the cultural and social heritage of Assam.

The RSS first transformed the agitation from being anti-bahiragat to being an anti-*videshi* (foreigners) movement. In gradual course of time, the sentiments were further directed against the immigrant Bangladeshis and later against the Bangladeshi Muslims. The question of saving the state's identity from the onslaught of foreign migrants echoed the nationalist and protectionist sentiment of the RSS. The then prominent ideologues of the RSS like Atal Bihari Vajpayee boldly took the Assam concern to the national fora, publicly and emphatically supporting the Assam Movement, in turn gaining popular sympathy and foothold in the state.

The Sangh gave a very shrewd but a well-articulated position on the migration question. After a series of meetings, in 1980, the RSS stated its opinion that Hindus were *sharanarthi*s (asylum) seekers and Muslims were *anupraveshkaari*s (infiltrators). RSS divided the migrants from Bangladesh into two groups. The first group consisted of Muslim migrants from Bangladesh to India, who had travelled to India in search of better economic opportunities. The RSS also claimed that this migration had been left unabated by the political establishment. It put forth the idea that this group fulfilled the political agenda of nursing and protecting a vote bank that could yield elections after elections in favour of its protector political party. The second group comprised the political refugees—the Hindu Bangladeshis. Being a minority in a Muslim dominated country, these migrants had fled their land and society in search of a refuge where they could respectfully follow their religion and live a life of dignity. Therefore, RSS cleverly delineated its position on the Bangladeshi migration issue. It took a severe position against the Muslim migrants, articulating its idea of selective protection to Hindu migrants in Assam.[9]

From an organization largely seen as a cultural, social and religious group of Vaishnavite *bhakts* (devotees), the RSS became the rallying point for all those victims whose land was forcibly taken away by the migrants, who were raped or molested at the hands of the new men in their area, who with civil and administrative manoeuvres acquired the lands of the satras and other cultural areas to set up their base.

The shift in the narrative of migration was a seminal point of departure in Assam's history. The consolidation of the Sangh as an organization growing stronger on the ideology of cultural assimilation led to many interesting events in the 1980s and 1990s. For example, the *ekmat yatra* (meant to mobilize the youth cadre of Assam in the service of the motherland) organized by the VHP was successful in Assam. The Parshuram Rath that travelled from Parshuramkunda in Arunachal Pradesh to Dhubri in Assam to Okha in Gujarat was also a successful exercise.

Therefore, the impact of the Assam Movement on the fulcrum of all political discussions in Assam is not surprising. There is nostalgia, a sense of pride, a sense of realization of the national impact this movement had and an acknowledgement that the movement during 1979–85 altered the destiny of Assam forever.

Interpreting Assam—the RSS Way

Being Hindu means different things to different groups of people, in various situations and lands. Because there is no single codified book, text, scripture, idea or tenet that defines Hindutva or Hinduism or Hindu way of life, each region defines a Hindu in its own way. The challenge for the RSS in Assam was to define, promote and entrench the term Hindu in the consciousness of the state in such a way that the local histories, myths, idioms and fables become a part of the Sangh's conception of a Hindu nationhood in Assam.

The aftermath of colonial projects and reorganization of political boundaries of Assam—internally and outside— with respect to Partition and the Bangladesh war and states reorganization, always kept the identity question alive in the state. Who belongs to Assam, who does Assam belong to, who can claim an access to the identity of Assam and who can identify with Assam are questions that keep repeating themselves in different ways at different points of time in Assam's historical imagination. Therefore, the burning question of identity in Assam provided a ready ground for the RSS to address this question and propose a possible answer.

The RSS attempted to define the link between Bharat and Assam. It went back to the religious, historical, quasi-historical and mythological accounts of Hinduism and India to resurrect those instances and anecdotes that linked this part of the country with the age-old concept of India as an integrated nation.

The references to Pragjyotishpur and Kamrup in the Vedic, Puranic and epic texts were recounted and repackaged to suit the modern conception of Assam. The cult of Shaivism, for example was redefined in the religious practices of the Bodoland. Vaishnavism found expression in Srimanta Sankardeva's heritage and was later popularized by ISCKON.

Shaktism manifested itself in the cult of Devi Kamakhya in the form of the *shaktipeeth* at Nilanchal in Guwahati. The Ahom kings from Rudra Singha onwards also embraced Hinduism and brought various tribes into the Hindu fold.

The fact that Sanskrit language is closer to Assamese also played a central role in narrating the mother–daughter relationship between the two languages. It instantly helped connect the two distinct identities that had been marred over by decades of mistrust. Ironically, in a state where language has always been a contested claim of conflict within identities, the Sangh used the *devbhasha* Sanskrit as a link to reconstruct Assam as a part of the larger rubric of the shared linguistic and cultural heritage of the Hindu *rashtra*.

Equally significant has been how the Sangh used the teachings of Srimanta Sankardeva to the advantage of unifying India and integrating Assam with Bharat. The fifteenth-to-sixteenth-century polymath Sankardeva left his house after the death of his wife for a tour of Bharatavarsha. When he returned to Assam after twelve years, he created the unique Eksarana Dharma tradition within the Vaishnavite cult, inspired by bhakti. By codifying a very simple and easily accessible form of worship that rejected complicated rites and rituals, Srimanta Sankardeva also created dance and music forms that went beyond just worship. He began the Sattriya dance form, and the *borgeet*s, *ankia naat*s and *bhaona*s (the new forms of Assamese music and theatre)—all of which have come to symbolize a tradition that is identified with Assam.

The RSS took shelter to grow in Assam under the satra tradition established by Sankardeva. Later, in 2000, RSS cultural artists and activists played an instrumental role in getting the

Sattriya dance form the national honour of being recognized as a classical dance form by the Sangeet Natak Akademi.

The cult of Sankardeva has been kept alive by the RSS and his teachings imparted via Sankardeva Shishu Kunjas,[10] which use Bengali and Assamese as the media of instruction in the Barak and Brahmaputra valleys, respectively. Similarly, the RSS runs Ekal Vidyalays—one teacher schools in tribal areas.

Apart from these routine social activities that the Sangh engages in, the ideological manoeuvring of the organization in a culturally rich yet distraught region like Assam is interesting. Identifying the criticality of the question of identity in Assam, RSS learnt early on that nationalism in Assam would not be relatable purely on the basis of a citizenship stamp. Identity question, being the key concern for the people of Assam, was a double-edged sword for the Sangh. On the one hand, the issue of identity could rally local support and gain acceptability of the RSS in Assam. On the other hand, support to the parochial claims could have undermined the nationalist agenda of the Sangh.

The challenge before the RSS was to widen the ambit of its nationalism. In order to subsume the Assamese identity into that of being an Indian, it had to first accept the diversity of identities in Assam, which were albeit united by the common identification of a regional entity. Second, it had to embrace the cultural aspects of identity which were plural, layered and multidimensional. This realization and the manifestation of this idea in the Sangh's posturing, work and commitments in Assam was central to marrying the idea of belonging to Assam with that of India. RSS imbibed and propagated local customs, local tales of heroism and valour, local traditions and rich tales of historical legacy and heritage to stitch the overarching national values of the organization. It should come as no surprise then that the war cry of the Last Battle of Saraighat to denote the magnanimity of the assembly elections 2016 had such a huge emotional appeal.

As an ideological offshoot of the RSS, if one looks at the BJP, one finds something unique about the party's style of politics. In spite of being branded as a polarizing political force, it has a secret recipe that allows it to bond well with strong regionalist, and in some cases, subnational satraps—be it the Shiv Sena in Maharashtra, the Peoples Democratic Party in Jammu and Kashmir or the AGP in Assam. This secret sauce of unification and subsuming of strong regional sentiments within the accommodative, national politics of the BJP is what opens up the practical possibilities of 'dream alliances'.

chapter four

GETTING BATTLE-READY

'The supreme art of war is to subdue the enemy without fighting.'

—Sun Tzu

~

Assam celebrates three different Bihu festivals, each one of which coincides with a distinct phase in the farming calendar. Kati Bihu, the first in the series, is observed in October and is marked by solemn prayers to save the paddy crop from insects and evil sights. Bhogali or Magh Bihu is all about food and is celebrated in January at the end of paddy harvesting period when the granaries are full. The last Bihu in the calendar is called Rongali Bihu or Bohag Bihu, which marks the beginning of the Assamese New Year when the field is prepared for the next season of paddy cultivation. It is the most widely celebrated and colourful festival in Assam.

Every five years, the Assamese farming calendar closely coincides with the campaign calendars of political parties. The body politic of Assam is promised new dreams every time. This interesting tradition was captured in a 1992 song by Bhupen Hazarika on Bihu. Sung to the tune of a lullaby, it makes a plea to Bihu: *Please do come once a year and wake up mother Assam, and even in these dangerous times, please O Bihu, come and give the Assamese body and mind its ritual bath.*

Bihu is indeed a 'national birthday—the day of renewal when the Assamese polity takes stock of its past and future'. In the Bihu of 2016, the electoral curtains were to drop and a new polity was to emerge.

Armouring for the Battle

By the end of December 2015, BJP had almost all the right ingredients in place to project itself as the sole and credible political challenger to the incumbent Congress government in the ensuing assembly elections scheduled for April 2016. Anti-incumbency against the Tarun Gogoi–led Congress government was quickly building up. The BJP now appeared stronger as an Opposition in Assam. It had a face. It had the narrative. The party also had the required momentum to oust the incumbent. But a deep emotional connect with the people of Assam was amiss. BJP had so far been only a marginal political player in the state and electorate were still finding it hard to relate with the party as its political choice.

On the other hand, the Congress had a well-oiled foundation and a veteran leader in Gogoi, who had led the state peacefully for fifteen long years. Assam has traditionally been a strong Congress bastion. Out of the nearly seven decades of independent India, the Congress was in power in Assam for nearly six decades. Winning Assam would have meant that the

Congress was able to hold on to its turfs after its decimation in the 2014 Lok Sabha elections. Losing Assam would have implied a nosedive for the party nationally.

With the political ground that the BJP had covered over the past two years, it could not afford to lose the Assam battle. The next four months of electioneering were critical to tilt the balance in its favour. After the humiliating defeat in Delhi and Bihar, Assam was a test of the BJP's confidence. It would also signify if there was a sense of trust for the party among the masses and if the Modi wave still reigned high in urban as well as far-flung rural centres of India. For the BJP, it meant finding a foothold in North-east India and marking its presence in a sensitive borderland. For the central government under Modi, Assam, if claimed, would have become a pivot for the Act East Policy. So, for all reasons—political and developmental—Assam was a catch!

Navigating the Complex Demographic Maze

As discussed in earlier chapters, Upper Assam was the seat of the Ahom kingdom which reigned for almost six centuries uninterrupted. The Ahoms and their politics completely dominated this region, especially the districts of Sibsagar, Jorhat and Dibrugarh. Another big demography that had settled in the region around the middle of the nineteenth century was that of the tea tribes working in the tea estates. The rest of the demography included plain tribal groups, such as Sonowal Kachari, Mishing, Motok and Moran. The Congress believed that it would be able to hold on to the Ahom fortress in Sibsagar and Jorhat because it was the stronghold of Tarun

Gogoi, who was himself an Ahom. BJP had its own set of Ahom leaders, but no one was as towering as Tarun Gogoi.

The BJP put up Sarbananda Sonowal as its major contender, who belongs to the socially weaker Sonowal Kachari tribe, against the princely Ahoms led by Gogoi. This move helped several small tribal groups come together in favour of the BJP, and the elections in Upper Assam were left in the hands of the tea tribes.

As an Assamese journalist describes—'you know you are in upper Assam by merely smelling the air. With roughly 800 tea gardens spread across the seven upper Assam districts of Jorhat, Golaghat, Sibsagar, Dibrugarh, Tinsukia, Lakhimpur and Dhemaji, the robust aroma of freshly plucked tea leaves is difficult to escape'.[1]

The manual labour required at these tea estates is the main source of employment for the state's tea tribes. Four generations of these tribes have now been living in the state. Only a few families have been able to emerge from the vicious circle of poverty in the estate and moved to other professions. Others are short on dreams. They have never experienced life out of the estates. Their daily schedules are micromanaged by estate managers, which even includes when they should eat and sleep. Demographically, the tea garden workers, ex-workers and their families account for up to 31 lakh people, or nearly 17 per cent of the state's population.[2]

The BJP's entire strategy of sweeping Upper Assam hinged on the support of tea tribes. Tea workers are in a position to influence the outcome of as many as sixty assembly constituencies and five parliamentary constituencies—

Kaliabor, Mangaldoi, Dibrugarh, Lakhimpur and Jorhat. In the run-up to the elections, the BJP invested substantial effort to further consolidate on the electoral progress it had made in the tea estates during the 2014 campaign. For the first time in the history of television in Assam, a TV commercial was broadcasted in the Santhali dialect prominently used by the tea tribes. This advertisement highlighted how for four generations of tea tribes, from the time when they first migrated to Assam till today, their lives have remained virtually unchanged. A century ago, they were plucking tea leaves for ten hours a day, and a century later, they do the very same for a similar number of hours each day. It was the reminder of this criminal neglect of incumbent regimes to improve the lives of tea tribes along with the well-constructed image of the prime minister as a tea seller that resulted in the windfall electoral gains for the BJP.

The Congress gradually realized that the dent in its traditional tea-tribe vote bank had become an irreversible political change. The only way for the party to penetrate this important vote bank was to exploit the complex relationship between the tea workers and estate managers. It, therefore, tried to arm-twist its way into regaining the lost ground by seeking help from the powerful tea estate owners' lobbies.

The relationship between the successive regimes of the Congress and estate owners had become ossified into a well-oiled symbiotic machinery. The owners—managers of the privately owned estates usually carry disproportionate influence on tea labourers. Estate managers are notorious for controlling the political narrative that dominates the region. Right from dictating which labour union they should join to

which political party to vote for—they have usurped the tea
tribes of their basic rights of free political expression for years.
They have so strictly regimented the day-to-day lives of tea
workers that from the time they wake up to the time they have
meal breaks—everything is codified. During the day of polls,
these managers deploy estate security to escort tea workers and
ensure that the workers vote en bloc for a particular candidate.

Breaking this stranglehold of the managerial clout was
indeed a challenge for the BJP. Years of dependence of the
tea estate workers on their *mai baap* (tea estate owners and
managers) had asphyxiated their voices. These workers needed
to find their voice as free citizens. And for this to happen
they needed a political movement that freed them from the
monopolistic powers of the ones above them.

The Assam Chah Mazdoor Sangh (ACMS), or the Assam Tea
Workers' Union, was among the most influential labour unions
in the region. Partly because of its affiliation with its parent
body—Indian National Trade Union Congress (INTUC) and
an open political affiliation with the Congress party, the ACMS
flourished with significant clout. The ACMS was set up by the
Dibrugarh Congress leader Mahabendra Nath Sharma and a
group of tea garden trade unionist leaders. An agreement was
reached between then Assam chief minister Gopinath Bordoloi,
INTUC and the Indian Tea Association (an association of tea
producers). The INTUC promised the plantation owners that
they will not engage in 'disruptive' union activism whilst the
Indian Tea Association promised the INTUC would be given
free access to unionizing the labour force in the tea gardens.[3]
Through this agreement with the tea plantation owners, the
ACMS was able to establish a virtual monopoly over organizing

labour in the Assam valley tea gardens. Gradually, it became a very important pillar for the Congress to hold on to power in Assam for several decades. The grapevines in the tea estates suggest that the labour union membership fees of a prominent labour union, which was collected mostly in cash from the tea labourers, was channelled to support the finances of the head office of one particular political party.

To break this monopolistic clout of ACMS, the Bharatiya Mazdoor Sangh (BMS), an RSS-affiliated labour union stepped in. Building a new tea workers' union from the ground up with little political support was indeed a Herculean task for BMS. While it did struggle to create a foothold in the tea gardens, it provided a test ground for a new politics to emerge and challenged the monopoly of the Congress-led ACMS by making workers aware of the opportunities they lost under successive Congress regimes vis-à-vis labourers in BJP-ruled states. The BMS constantly reminded tea workers how their labour unions and elected governments betrayed them and went back on their promises of providing basic living amenities under the Plantation Labour Act of 1951.

This awakening, accompanied with Modi's aggressive co-option of the sentiments of tea workers, stitched a crucial electoral mandate in favour of the BJP. 'Also, if you talk about the tea garden community in particular, there is a fatigue factor in ACMS, particularly among the youth which comprises 40 per cent of that community's voters. This is the aspirational class, they want to educate themselves, compete for jobs, so they want a change of government this time. They are unlikely to go with Congress yet again,' says Nani Gopal Mahanta, Gauhati University's political science professor and well-known political commentator.

BJP's Bengali Conundrum

Assam's southern tail constitutes the Barak river valley, comprising of three districts—Cachar, Karimganj and Hailakandi, and shares border with Bangladesh. It has fifteen seats in the 126-member Assam assembly. In the 2011 assembly elections, the Congress won thirteen seats while the BJP failed to win a single seat. The AGP and the AIUDF won one seat each. In 2014, the Modi wave swept the Brahmaputra valley but did not have much impact on the Barak valley. The valley has two Lok Sabha seats—Silchar and Karimganj. In the 2014 Lok Sabha polls, the Congress wrested the Silchar seat from the BJP but lost the Karimganj seat to AIUDF. The Congress polled the highest votes in seven assembly segments, the AIUDF in five and the BJP in three segments in 2014.

Why did the BJP never fare well in Barak valley? It was probably because it never completely understood the polity of the region. Just as the region is disconnected from the mainland Assam geographically, similarly in its politics, it is disconnected from the mainstream politics of Assam. The BJP did not invest enough energy in understanding the sentiments of the people from the region. The politics of the Bengali-speaking Barak valley is entangled in a complex zero-sum game with the politics of the mainland, Assamese-speaking part of Assam. What was being said in the election rallies in Upper Assam would rub people the wrong way in the Barak valley. For instance, the clarion call to safeguard *jaati* (nation), *maati* (land) and *bheti* (house) touches the emotional chord of citizens of the Brahmaputra valley. On the other hand, the predominantly Bangladeshi immigrants who form the Bengali-speaking population in Barak valley are seen as a direct threat to the jaati–maati–bheti, hence the slogan cannot be invoked there. Similarly, any protection of political interests of the Bengalis irks the Assamese-speaking population.

This direct confrontation between the sociopolitical issues of the Barak valley and the Brahmaputra valley makes the political balancing act a complex and nuanced exercise that requires time and patience to cultivate. Over the years, the Congress had perfected the art of carefully projecting itself as the saviour of the two insecure social groups—Bengali Hindus and Bengali-speaking Muslims along with winning the votes of specific communities to reach the magic number.

More than local development concerns, the matter that captivated the people in the Barak region was the foreign policy of India vis-à-vis Bangladesh. During the election, the BJP heavily banked on the two notifications issued by the Narendra Modi–led NDA government under the Passport (Entry into India) Act, 1920, and the Foreigners Act, 1946, which gave official assurance of providing shelter to Bangladeshi Hindus fleeing to India due to alleged persecution in the neighbouring country. According to the official press release by the home affairs ministry on 7 September 2015, 'The Central Government has decided, on humanitarian considerations, to exempt Bangladeshi and Pakistani nationals belonging to minority communities who have entered into India on or before 31 December 2014 from the relevant provisions of rules and order made under the Passport (Entry into India) Act, 1920, and the Foreigners Act, 1946 . . . There are reports that a number of Bangladeshi and Pakistani nationals belonging to minority communities in those countries, such as Hindus,

Sikhs, Christians, Jains, Parsis and Buddhists, were compelled to seek shelter in India due to religious persecution or fear of religious persecution.'[4] This ordinance, which later was brought to the Parliament for deliberations as the Citizenship Bill 2016, helped legalize the citizenship status of Hindu Bengalis in Assam. BJP's campaign machine for Barak valley was designed aggressively to gain maximum electoral advantage from the region.

The Congress's reaction to this electoral strategy of BJP was an expected one. It brought in the secular–communal debate and revived its national level strategy of positing itself on its 'secular' credentials as opposed to the 'communal' BJP. In our understanding, the Congress wanted to position the NDA government in the Centre as selectively granting citizenship to Bangladeshi Hindus and denying similar humanitarian provisions to Bangladeshi Muslims through its Citizenship Amendment Bill. The Congress would have also wanted to position the BJP as going against the core essence of the Assam Accord—by granting citizenship to Bangladeshi migrants. We thought this strategy had little chance of succeeding. While the Bengali Muslim electorates were generally not enthused by the Congress, because while in government it had done little for their social security, to the Assamese people, who could have reacted adversely against BJP's stand on legalizing the status of Bangladeshi Hindu immigrants, the Congress was seen as safeguarding the interests of Bangladeshi Muslim immigrants. Hence, the Congress was in a fix—if it opposed the ordinance it would lose significant seats in the Barak valley; if it supported the move, it would lose an opportunity to corner BJP and gain the sympathy of the Assamese electorate. The Congress chose to position itself where the politics of Badruddin Ajmal stood—standing with the cause of Muslim migrants. What could have cost the BJP dearly in the Brahmaputra valley couldn't be made an effective electoral issue. It was the sheer force of BJP's electioneering that kept the focus of the Assamese people on the move against the Bangladeshi migrants and also convinced Hindu Bengalis that the BJP was serious about safeguarding their interest.

Being BJP: A Challenge

The BJP is, by and large, understood as a cow belt party, whose politics seems disconnected with the regional realities of a state like Assam with its social complexities. By using the phrase 'cow belt' and repeating it ad nauseam in Assam, the Opposition had somehow established that the BJP as a party does not gel in with the Assamese ethos. It was painted as a party of the outsiders and by the outsiders who had come to 'Hinduize' Assam. This created a monolithic image of the BJP as filled with people who speak Hindi, have no regard for diversity and have no idea about the cultural traditions and heritage of Assam. Some of this perception was consolidated by statements made by BJP national leaders in the state. Mahendra Singh, BJP national secretary and in-charge of Assam, had referred to Srimanta Sankardeva as 'Baba' Sankardeo during a public rally. This was enough ammunition for Gogoi: 'If BJP leaders did not know about the Mahapurusha, what can Assam expect from them,' he asked. 'Let the BJP leaders first know about the great saint-social reformer and his ideals before they can think of doing something in his honour,' he said.[5] Gogoi branded Singh an 'outsider trying to invade the state with Hindigri'.[6]

The challenge for the BJP was multifold. Fresh from the defeat in the assembly elections in Delhi and Bihar, the leaders were aggressive, morose and trying to find their feet on an uncharted turf. The Congress openly made fun of the BJP's performance in Bihar and it added insult to injury. Besides, the death of Akhlaq in Dadri, Uttar Pradesh, over a beef controversy was raging so high in the media that the Congress had got enough resources and ammunition to start misinformation campaigns and negative publicity on the ground against the BJP. The BJP leadership realized this early on in the campaign and course corrected several times.

The daunting task ahead was to somehow balance the narrative, establish a face for the party, appear fresh for the electoral battle, make the party localized and attuned to a different kind of politics needed in Assam at that time. It was important to first find a binding, subliminal voice that would sustain the campaign fever. And this voice had to be something beyond the regular *roti*, *kapda*, *makaan* concerns.

The usual cry about civic amenities and issues, which is the bulk of election rhetoric in India, does not garner much support. Because of the repetition of issues that have not been solved ever since we have had an independent political system, this appeal for basic amenities has become an issue that does not evoke any emotion. Despite the huge anti-incumbency against the fifteen years of Tarun Gogoi's government, this appeal could have taken the BJP, at the maximum, to around thirty-five to forty seats. Breaking this threshold and taking the party to more than sixty seats required garnering the votes of every big and small community in the state. The BJP realized that in order to secure an independent majority, there was a need for an appeal that moved not just the mind but also the hearts of the people. It was equally significant to shun the hubris of a grand, national agenda and localize itself. And finally, it was necessary to tone down the aggression and respond with mature ease in a new avatar. In order to win decisively in a state like Assam where starting numbers did not do justice to the aspirations of the BJP, the party needed a wave. And waves can only be built on deep emotive connect with the electorate.

Going for the Kill

Assam is mini India by the sheer diversity and the sheer expanse of the state. Each geographical unit of the state expresses a different culture, cuisine, sartorial sense, tradition, faith and other markers of a rich heritage. Also, one part of the state is not friendly with the other, tribes are always in conflict with each other, there is linguistic politics, there is competitive identity politics at play and of course there are severe inequalities and civic issues.

It was important to understand the various parts and contours of the state. It was important to learn what not to speak where rather than just be adept at speaking on issues. In this respect, before one learnt to craft communication strategies, it was important to deeply connect with the state.

After this initial round of study was done and ground surveys looked at, the first line of communication was attempted at projecting tribal and non-tribal unity as the BJP's conceptualization of Assam. In contrast with the already divided atmosphere created by the Congress, this communication came as a breath of fresh air. Besides, it also allayed the manufactured fears about the BJP being a divisive party. In its first set of hoardings, the BJP put forth representations from different communities holding hands together offering their gratitude to Axomi Aai (Mother Assam). The one line message was— '*Matrabhoomi tomak namaskar* [Motherland, I bow in front of you].' With this first public message, the BJP launched itself with sharp regionalist overture.

Later, in subsequent rounds, the BJP came down heavily on the Congress government and Tarun Gogoi's rule in Assam in its political messaging. Questions of rampant corruption, lack of basic infrastructure and unfinished projects were directed from all channels of communication. The communication was meant to be direct and accusatory. The intent was to stoke anti-incumbency to its maximum level before shifting to project more hopeful messages.

While the communication was being sharpened at BJP's Guwahati war room, the party leadership planned to build a strong network of party workers to carry its political message to each household. The target was fixed. The BJP had to dethrone the reigning Congress and win eighty-four seats out of 126 seats in Assam. It won sixty-nine assembly-equivalent seats in the 2014 Lok Sabha elections and stood second in fifteen seats. Targeting these prospective seats, the party launched its ambitious 'Mission 84'.

The BJP began with a registered membership of 3,50,000 in November 2014. The state had a total of 24,000 polling booths. Bringing one hundred members into the fold of the party in each booth would have set the target at 2.4 million members. The state leadership was given this target. A Maha Sampark Abhiyan (Grand Outreach Programme) was initiated. From missed calls to online registrations, including meeting many youths personally, state leaders helped the party gain a strong foothold in the state.

While Assam is known to be the land of '*lahe lahe*' (translating to 'slow slow'), where things move at a slow pace, such daunting targets seemed a long shot. Several leaders in private discussions shared that such lofty goals were meant to be just an academic exercise. Many confided that the BJP should be happy being the main opposition party post the 2016 assembly results. In spite of such acute lack of self-belief, the state functionaries kept their focus on the micro targets set out for each of them. The party created *mandal* in-charges, district in-charges, booth in-charges. In less than eighteen months, BJP's membership touched 3.1 million, much beyond the expected targets. The party also started the Maha-Prasikshan Abhiyan (Grand Training Programme) that trained its booth-level functionaries to spread the good work done by the central government led by Modi. They were delegated specific responsibilities of reaching each household once a week with a different message.

The organizational behemoth was ready to move in for the final kill.

Reading the Congress's Mind

Few journalists have shown the courage to understand, interpret and boldly put forth the designs employed by the Congress to win elections. Arun Shourie has been an exception in this regard. While covering the 1983 Assam assembly elections, marred by the worst communal violence the nation had ever experienced, Shourie lamented, 'The electoral strategy of the party [Congress] was the familiar one: isolate the largest group; gather together the other groups; foment insecurity in them; and then present yourself as the only available protector.'[7] Three decades down the timeline, little has evolved in the Congress's strategy of winning elections in Assam and elsewhere.

Devkanta Barooah was the Congress president during the Emergency (1975–77). A supreme Indira Gandhi loyalist, he rose to fame for coining the phrase—'Indira is India, India is Indira'. When it came to phraseology, few contemporary politicians could beat him. Few people outside of Assam know that he created the most electorally relevant phrase—'Ali–Kuli–Bengali'—a formula that helped the Congress cling to power in Assam for decades. Ali stands for Bengali speaking Muslims settled by the British along the riverbanks, mostly for paddy and vegetable cultivation. Kuli refers to Adivasis brought from central India to work in tea plantations and as loggers for the timber trade. The British relied on 'Bongalis', or Bengali Hindus, for clerical jobs and petty trade. The Congress had mastered the electoral strategy of making itself the sole electoral choice for these segments of society by politically nurturing them over the years. They invariably stood by the Congress, even in the 1985 elections held in the aftermath of the Assam Movement when the party slipped to its lowest tally of twenty-five seats. Together, these communities have dictated the outcome in ninety of Assam's 126 assembly seats. Bengali Muslims hold sway over forty seats, Adivasis in thirty, and Bengali Hindus in ten.

The Ali

By 2015, the Congress had realized that it had lost its monopoly over the critical Muslim vote bank. In a little over a decade, perfume baron Badruddin Ajmal's AIUDF had eaten into the migrant Muslim vote base of the Congress. Ajmal was seen as a more credible face by the Muslims for the enormous development work he had done for the community in his home constituency of Hojai. The then chief minister Tarun Gogoi, eyeing a fourth straight term, claimed that the Congress had 'never really lost them [the Muslim voters]'.[8]

But deep down, Gogoi realized that Ajmal had made an irreversible dent on the Muslim vote bank. However, to side with the Maulana in an electoral alliance was a politically challenging and fraught decision. The exclusionary politics of the Maulana which focused on the minority vote bank, especially that of the Bangladeshi Muslims, made him an unlikely political coalition partner. Joining hands with him came with a communal tag, something that mainstream parties like the Congress did not want to overtly associate with. However, the AIUDF was a strong force with an air of invincibility in many constituencies of the state. The party had been consistently increasing its vote base and the assembly seats from its inception in 2006 right up to the 2014 Lok Sabha elections. In 2006, it had won ten assembly seats, eighteen seats in 2011 and three critical parliamentary seats in 2014. A Congress and AIUDF alliance would have been a formidable combination, but the fear it generated was also a stark reality.

The Kuli

As discussed earlier, the BJP had made deep inroads into the tea belt of Assam. It had cultivated new leaders, new organizations and a fresh political message to appeal to the tea workers. In 2014, it had won the crucial seats of Dibrugarh and Jorhat. The Congress had little time in hand to turn the tide in its favour. It appears that the Congress's line of campaign in the tea belt for this election was to focus voters' attention on the Modi government's failure to improve the lives of tea garden workers. It seems that they planned to highlight how the prime minister often appreciates Assam tea and says that he used to sell Assam tea, and yet, is not aware of the pathetic condition of the tea garden workers in Assam. The Congress very well knew that the two most critical things that impact the daily lives of tea workers are—his or her daily wage and the subsidized ration given to them. The Gogoi government—in a shrewd move— right before the model code for the elections notified a draft proposal to enhance the minimum wage for both temporary and permanent tea plantation workers to Rs 177.19 from the measly Rs 115. For years, tea workers had been lamenting about their low daily wages, lower than the standards set by the rural employment guarantee scheme MNREGA. It was only at the turn of the elections that the Congress government thought this executive order might help it to salvage its deteriorating base among tea workers. Instead of solving anything, this order created havoc. The tea industry, facing global competitive pressures, was not ready to support a 50 per cent jump in the tea worker wages in one go. The order also touched the raw nerves of the workers who had been fighting lone battles against the might of the tea estate owners. The dilly-dallying of the government on this decision created confusion in the minds of a significant voting class of tea workers.

During its campaign, the Congress tried to use the classic strategy—if you cannot convince, confuse. Congress workers started spreading rumours that the Modi government would suspend the 35-kg subsidized wheat and rice the tea workers are entitled to. In one of the interactions with a rickshaw driver in Guwahati, the effect of this rumour-mongering was visibly clear.

The rickshaw driver, who was inebriated, was helping his wife set up the evening vegetable stall in Hengrabari. He was so drunk that he could barely stand. On being asked about the political situation in Assam, the wife began to talk about how change is needed from a government that has done practically nothing in the last fifteen years. The driver cut her short and said that despite the fact that he hopes the government changes, he will not vote for the BJP this time around. He continued that there is information that once the BJP comes to power it will roll back the ration provision to the poor.

Tea workers are heavily dependent on ration as they cannot afford the food grains from the market. Even a mere thought of suspension of food ration was enough to create panic. As per her party's script, Sonia Gandhi, addressing a public rally in Amguri in Sibsagar district a day after Singh and Sarma's visits, highlighted these issues: 'The country wakes up with Assam tea. He suspended twelve schemes meant for poor, one of which has stopped free ration received by the tea garden workers during our government. The tea garden workers in Assam are still wondering as to when the "*achche din*" [good days] will come in their lives,' Gandhi said.[9] As the rumour spread like a wildfire, the BJP's rank and file soon realized the huge impact this could have on the coming elections. Who else than Modi was better suited to allay such fears! Prime Minister Modi, on realizing the magnitude of the problem, clarified in his public speeches that his government had no intent to dilute the food rationing provided to the tea workers under the food security act.

Apart from misinformation campaigns, prior to elections, the Congress announced three new schemes for the tea plantation workers. Under the Bagan Ghar Scheme, every tea plantation worker's family was to be provided with land and financial assistance to construct a dwelling. Bagan Jal scheme promised to provide drinking water in the labour lines. Bagan Bus Scheme was rolled out to provide public bus service to the school and college going children of the tea plantation workers. Apart from this last minute policy formulation, in order to publicize some action on the ground, the state government distributed land *pattas* to some landless workers.

On the one hand, the Congress sharpened its electoral rhetoric around issues that deeply concerned the tea region population, while on the other hand it tried to offer a credible leadership and a face. The party decided to bank on the ACMS president Pawan Singh Ghatowar, a veteran Congress leader. A five-time Lok Sabha member of the Congress from Dibrugarh and a former Union minister, Ghatowar was the most prominent face from the tea community. Congress central leadership wanted to see Ghatowar's face help consolidate the tea garden vote. They were ready to toy with the idea of projecting him for the top job in the post-Gogoi era.

Congress vice president Rahul Gandhi emphasized the importance of these three important communities—the Ali, Kuli and Bengali—by addressing rallies, first in the Muslim-dominated Barpeta district of western Assam, the tea-growing belts of eastern Assam, and the Bengali Hindu-dominated Silchar in southern Assam.

Suta–Kambal–Athua Politics

The 'suta–kambal–athua' politics of the Congress has been yet another low-risk, high-returns-yielding strategy of the party for years, showcasing how it has been giving away free doles of weaving thread, blankets and mosquito nets to the poor every time electoral bells ring. Many trucks of suta–kambal line up outside the district collector's offices to be distributed to all and sundry. The party knows that these populist schemes have a lot of takers. This time the kambals prominently displayed Gogoi government's branding, leaving little to the imagination what they were meant for. Ask any politically aware Assamese and they will tell you what suta–kambal means for the politics in the state. 'BJP's main political opponent is suta–kambal, not Gogoi!' said a *gaon bora* (village head) in Biswanath Chariali.[10]

While the BJP wanted to stay focused on its election agenda of '*Vikas, charo taraf vikas, tej gati se vikas* [Development, all-round development, fast-paced development],' it also recognized the sheer vote-creation power of 'suta–kambal–athua' in Assam. Abstaining from using freebies for easy returns was indeed difficult for the BJP.

Suta–kambal is symptomatic of everything that has been wrong with the politics of the North-east. The people of Assam have been duped election after election with cheap freebies to buy their votes, and once they are bought, they lose the moral compass to question their elected representatives on the legislative work done by them. An average cost is calculated to buy each voter and varies greatly from one North-eastern state to another. In Arunachal Pradesh, the common belief is that each vote is bought out at the rate of ten thousand rupees. The massive electoral spends are later recovered through unparalleled levels of corruption. For decades, humongous amounts of money have been pumped into the seven states of the North-east for development work. Ideally, it should have resulted in big improvements in development indices. Unfortunately, most of it gets siphoned off. For instance, in Assam itself, the Comptroller and Auditor General, in 2015, observed that over a period of fifteen years, the state government had failed to provide answers to various inspection reports and not furnished utilization certificates, resulting in a loss to the state exchequer to the tune of Rs 1,80,000 crore.[11] Such mismanagement of the state's finances has kept the global and Indian investors away from the North-east in general and Assam in particular.

Make It a Modi versus Gogoi Battle

In an interview to a leading newspaper in Delhi,[12] Tarun Gogoi remarked that his electorate fight in Assam was against Modi and that this election was about a direct confrontation between a chief minister and the prime minister, between the contesting philosophies, effectiveness of development and governance model of the two leaders. The newspaper quoted Gogoi saying, 'The ensuing Assembly elections will be a showdown between me and Prime Minister Narendra Modi and the NDA Government's failure on all fronts and its anti-people and anti-poor policies will be his main poll planks.'

This assertion by Gogoi was more to do with his strategy rather than his politics. In the recent past, Indian politics has seen ups and downs in ways that were unimaginable a decade ago. Personality and cult politics have been increasingly replacing ideological battle mines and developmental agendas. Talk of progress, equality and other abstract notions are increasingly being used as a topping rather than the main ingredient, more as a token issue to enhance the personality cult than be the defining moment of the poll pitch. Some leaders have been able to sell this quite well and won successive electoral mandates, for example, Mamata Banerjee in West Bengal or the late Jayalalithaa in Tamil Nadu.

Tarun Gogoi was of the same league. We believe that by pitting himself against Prime Minister Modi, Gogoi tried to kill several birds in one stroke. First, in his fight with Modi he could dismiss the local BJP leadership as irrelevant. Second, he could make it an insider versus outsider battle, an Axomiya standing up to the might of an outsider. Third, such comparisons could allow Gogoi to cover his failings and distract the electorate from the high degree of anti-incumbency. Fourth, pulling Modi into the election rhetoric could make the election a referendum of two years of his rule at the Centre rather than fifteen years of Gogoi rule. A potential win for the Congress in Assam might have been important as the last strike on the Modi regime after the defeats of Delhi and Bihar—something that would render him powerless. A Modi versus Gogoi battle, we believe, would have benefitted the Congress. The BJP made considerable efforts to use local faces to counter Gogoi. The BJP made a conscious effort to protect the image of Modi and use it selectively and strategically.

Back to Basics

The Congress was banking on its workers' strength on the ground. It had a time-tested robust network of booth-level workers mapped out well in advance. The Congress entered the 2016 poll race with seventy-eight sitting MLAs. Led by Himanta Biswa Sarma, ten MLAs defected to the BJP around August 2015. In spite of the setback, the Congress still had a clear advantage in terms of a disciplined organizational base as compared to the BJP. On the other hand, the BJP had only five MLAs in the outgoing assembly. Its organization was in tatters. The factions in the BJP had almost vertically split the party into two halves. Several districts were running two parallel offices. With little clarity about the leadership at every level of the organization, no one expected the BJP to stand up to the organizational might of the Congress party. With the departure of Himanta Biswa, the leadership question in the Congress was put to rest at least for the coming elections and Tarun Gogoi seemed firmly in command of the party.

Maulana: The Political Pariah

The AIUDF, headed by Maulana Badruddin Ajmal, is a regional party in Assam. Maulana is a Lok Sabha MP from Dhubri constituency. He founded the AIUDF which bagged ten seats in its maiden electoral fight in the 2006 assembly elections. Later, in 2011, the party garnered eighteen seats and emerged as the largest opposition party in Assam.

The AIUDF is known for its pro-migrants stand. With the question of migration being a delicate political issue in the state ever since Assam came into being, our reading has been that no political party supports Badruddin Ajmal and his party openly. We believe that he and his party have been pariahs in Assam for the stand they openly endorse and take.

The universal and unilateral support that the Assam Movement garnered against the illegal occupation of land, jobs and culture, cut across all lines of class, gender and age. Since the movement took place fairly recently in history, the emotions that led to the movement are still apparent among the people. Frustration at the outcomes of the movement not being as desired and a general sense of disillusionment with the political landscape within the state and beyond is palpable under the surface. The youth who led the movement from the front or some who were part of the movement are still engaged in politics today and have matured and aged. Some of these include former chief minister Prafulla Mahanta, Kesab Mahanta, Chandra Mohan Patowary, etc. Their fidelity to the core issue of the movement still remains. Especially with demographic changes continuing unabated, the issue of migration still remains a concern. Therefore, Maulana's open advocacy for the migrants does not quite go down well with the Assamese society at large.

The latest census data[13] reveals a steep rise in the migrant population in nine border districts of Assam. In some cases, the population has exceeded 80 per cent. The AIUDF quickly transformed into a formidable political force within the span of a decade. After a solid performance in the 2014 parliamentary elections and having bagged three Lok Sabha seats, Badruddin then set his eyes upon the 2016 assembly elections. He was convinced that he would emerge as the king maker in Assam politics and no political party would be able to form a government in Dispur without his support.

However, there was always an apprehension among the mainstream political parties to side with the Maulana and his politics. In fact, during the last assembly elections in Assam (2011), cashing in on anti-migrant sentiments, the Congress played a polarizing card and Tarun Gogoi led the refrain of, 'Who is Badruddin?', discrediting Maulana and his hold on Assam. Reflecting popular Assamese sentiment, which did not quite reckon with AIUDF's politics, the Congress won a historic majority battling ten years of anti-incumbency. However, Maulana had consolidated his hold on the ten seats it had won earlier and expanded it across eighteen out of 126 assembly constituencies.

Therefore, the significance of the AIUDF in Assam was something that could not be ignored during the 2016 assembly elections. At the same time, with the BJP growing strong and anti-incumbency looming large on the Congress, Tarun Gogoi felt it was an opportune time to start reaching out to the AIUDF for an alliance. But, aware of the political unviability of the Maulana and wary of public reaction, the parties kept the talks within wraps till the end of the second phase of elections. However, the Congress never came out in the open to suggest an alliance with the AIUDF. There were hints being dropped but the parties went on record to say that they would fight the election alone. It was only later that the

Maulana opened up on Twitter about the possible alliance with the Congress which could not materialize because of Tarun Gogoi's wishy-washy attitude.

The plank of identity politics that the BJP used to its advantage was amplified by extraneous factors that further strengthened the party's position. Every political rally the Maulana addressed, he talked about the need to either vote for the AIUDF or the Congress in case AIUDF did not field its candidates in that constituency. Unlike the 2011 campaign when Tarun Gogoi openly declared, 'Who is Badruddin Ajmal?' in order to draw attention to the Congress's distance from the Maulana, this time around, Gogoi never openly denounced Ajmal. Rather, the Congress and Gogoi repeatedly gave conflicting statements with respect to the alliance.

The BJP turned this lack of clarity into an opportunity for itself. It swore allegiance to the jaati, maati, bheti of Assam, and not just distanced itself from the AIUDF and Maulana but also managed to convey that the only way to vote against the Congress was to vote for the BJP.

Jai Aai Axom and Bharat Mata Ki Jai: A Rainbow Alliance

The BJP, which had hitherto remained politically confined to some urban centres in Assam, wanted to expand its reach to the underbelly of the state. It wanted to redesign itself as a political force that represented pan-Assamese interests. Led by Ram Madhav, the party decided to stitch together various political splinter groups into a rainbow alliance. It planned to bring together various small and big tribal communities like the Bodos, the Rabhas, the Tiwas, the Mishings, the Sutiyas, the

Motoks and the Morans together in one political formation—an alliance that could challenge the electoral might of the Congress. In order to achieve that it was essential to have the AGP on its side. Both the AGP and the BJP had been in an alliance even in the past, so their coming together wouldn't be a surprise. However, the political negotiations between the two parties over the seat-sharing formula had stretched for far too long.

The AGP was split in two factions—the faction led by Prafulla Mahanta wanted to side with the Congress, the other faction led by Atul Bora was in favour of allying with the BJP. Behind the garb of the alliance question, the party was struggling with a bigger leadership question. Bora, who had recently taken the reigns of the party in his hands, had worked hard to rebuild the party cadre. Mahanta represented the old guard in the AGP desperate to regain the top post in the event the AGP could cobble up the numbers. He believed that both the BJP and the AGP were competing for the same electoral base. An alliance with the BJP could have ended the future relevance of AGP. However, both Atul Bora and Sarbananda Sonowal had served as the president of the AASU and therefore had good chemistry.

The internal dynamics of both these parties did not allow the possibility of an alliance. For far too long, the BJP state leaders rejected any collaboration, calling it a fatal strategy to infuse life into an almost-dead elephant—elephant being the party symbol of the AGP. The AGP, on the other hand, confident about its hold on its core vote base, especially in Upper Assam, did not want to concede ground. It wanted a significant number of seats for itself in the alliance formulation to satisfy its political aspirations.

The perception was that the AGP was a party that people believed had betrayed the aspirations of the people of Assam while in power—especially during its second term. This gave the BJP a clear edge above others. People wanted to try a new party that offered hope and did not have the baggage of betrayal. The public wanted to demand *poriborton* (change), from all the alternatives they had tried before. In that list of probable winners, the BJP knew it had an advantage. However, besides this advantage, the BJP had the opportunity to form a giant alliance of the regional forces and take the AGP on board to project itself as a national party that united people and was sensitive to their concerns. It was imperative to ensure that the perception of a credible opposition to the Congress in the BJP was strengthened and the effect stretched out on ground with enough electoral numbers and political support base. The numbers suggested the obvious speculation—an alliance between the AGP and the BJP—as the face of a united opposition to challenge the Congress–AIUDF coalition.

It was late in February when the stalemate on the alliance talks started frustrating the BJP. If it couldn't succeed in forging the partnership, it would have split the AGP vertically. Hints of an alliance between the AIUDF and the Congress gave the AGP and the BJP a reason to come closer. The identity question had always been a vexed issue in Assam. In the event of a possible alliance between the AIUDF and the Congress, the AGP could not have afforded to be seen as a part of such an alliance. Finally, a practical resolution emerged out of the political sagacity and numeric wisdom. On 2 March, the breakthrough was achieved and the BJP–AGP decided to go into a pre-poll alliance. The

AGP was offered the opportunity to contest twenty-four seats out of 126. The AGP decided to further contest for six seats in a 'friendly contest' with the BJP.

Realizing the futility of contesting alone in a situation as polarized as above, the BJP and the AGP had come together. For this election to be fought as the Last Battle of Saraighat, all small and big political forces had to come together under one umbrella. The coalition of all parties claiming to represent *khilonjiya* (indigenous front) was a political craft executed to perfection by Ram Madhav. He was successful in subsuming the radical parochial positions of various constituent parties within the larger narrative of ethnic nationalism.

When Prime Minister Modi came down to Assam to kick-start the intense phase of the campaign, all representatives of the constituent groups adorned the stage. Each leader ended their speech with 'Jai Aai Axom' and 'Bharat Mata ki jai'. The reverberations of the two salutations coming out together had deep political and ideological implications.

Campaign Insights

During elections, getting the narrative right from the beginning and trying to stick to not more than two to three basic messages is an ideal strategy for any party. Public perception and sustenance of the message can be ensured and strengthened by campaigns and outreach programmes that amplify the effect of the select few messages. But idealism hardly stays in the heat of elections. More often than not, communication during elections are pre-emptive, reactive and responsive. But it always helps to have the focus plank of the strategy defined right at the outset of the election cycle.

Government PR machinery

It has been observed that increasingly disproportionate amounts of public money is being spent on government publicity programmes on the eve of elections. These programmes essentially help push the publicity campaigns of the ruling political dispensation at the altar of the taxpayers' money. All political parties are complicit in this unethical malpractice. Unfortunately, the system fails the citizens here. The Model Code of Conduct is enforced a few weeks prior to elections, so the targeted poll campaigns prior to the Model Code of Conduct coming into effect do not come under legal scrutiny. It is deeply unfortunate that crores of government money and resources are spent on publicity rather than the delivery of schemes prior to seeking votes. Awareness drives on populist schemes launched by the government, selling of success stories by the government machinery and public outreach for feedback is all meant to convince the people cum voters in favour of the ruling party and also collect important public data with clear partisan political benefits.

For instance, the Bihar government launched the Badh Chala Bihar campaign, less than a year prior to the state assembly elections in 2015. Similarly, in Assam, the then state government led by the Congress initiated a public outreach programme to the estimated tune of a little less than Rs 50 crore prior to the assembly elections.

The Initial Lead of the Congress

By November 2015, the Congress had established its position in the minds of the voters. The publicity campaign launched by the Congress-run state government eight months prior to the elections in the state painted the entire state with a bold message on hoardings, speaking of the Congress's fifteen years of trust and development.

The Congress was in a positive frame of mind then and the hoardings, which adorned the national highways and prime locations in the city until December were marked by optimistic confidence and a sense of visible relaxation. White boards with bold, clear messages spoke of a government and party pretty much confident of being the only well-wisher of the public. The neatness and clarity of this slogan had caught up fast and had begun to stay on people's minds.

Admittedly, the Congress party had won the perception battle during the beginning of the campaign. They had managed to convey quite well that they alone enjoyed the trust and goodwill of the people of Assam. This was a very clever communication strategy.

The moment the Congress started out by asserting that it enjoyed a familiar camaraderie with the people it governed, it immediately occupied an intimate space of acceptance, albeit forced, among the minds of the electorate. A repetition of this message of knowingness and emotion of people's trust for over fifteen years over the entire length of the campaign would have really helped the Congress establish a credible face in the wake of huge anti-incumbency. But somehow, the focus got lost. As the events and the Congress's communication strategy unfolded, the narrative on the Congress's side faded from confidence to confusion to causticity to conclusive concession.

In the end, when the Congress chose to build on this message of familiarity by announcing Tarun Gogoi as *'aapun aapun laage'* or 'he is one of us' in its radio advertisements, the message had diluted to such a degree that it appeared more as a desperate attempt than anything else.

Confusion in the BJP Camp

While the Congress was gaining ground and traction in the initial few months of the campaign, the BJP was busy getting its house in order. The party coffers were dry. There was huge infighting within the various units of the party right from the top of the state leadership to the bottom rungs of the organization. In the wake of doing something rather than nothing, every leader came up with their own set of communication on the campaign and started putting it out.

However, hitting out at the incumbent government on charges of corruption, lack of good governance etc. were mundane messages that would have been oft repeated anywhere else by any opposition party. The need was to crystallize the poll campaign around one or two core issues of the electorate, which could rally sentiments and garner an en bloc, en masse appeal for a party. But for a party that appeared like a house divided in the beginning, it was far-fetched to think of a cohesive message on campaign strategies.

All this was really affecting the confidence of the party *karyakarta*s (party workers). Besides, the poll debacles in Bihar and Delhi had also lowered their morale. At this point in time, the BJP looked like a hassled group of politicians who were worried about not being able to reach out to the electorate due to lack of resources and most definitely political wisdom. The fear of losing out on communicating with the masses was palpable in every karyakarta.

Social Media: Filling in the Gaps

However, the fear and lackadaisical political temperature within the party did not extend to the online volunteers. Though divided on internal organizational issues, the online supporters of the BJP in Assam raged a huge Twitter and Facebook war. Every post by the Congress was torn into shreds by questions and counter claims. Even on Twitter, the then chief minister Tarun Gogoi was subjected to pointed questions on corruption, misgovernance and incompetent leadership. Additionally, the BJP managed to put out the ugly reality of the fifteen years of Congress rule with the hashtags #15YearsOfLoot and #15YearsOfCorruption, peppered with hard data, anecdotal evidence and crowd-sourced information from various constituencies.[14]

The social media spat between the two camps heightened the political mood within the state and ruffled feathers within the Congress camp. Despite emerging victorious in the perception battle on the streets, the Congress was rattled by this frontal attack on social media. All that the campaign teams in the BJP could not put out in the open on gigantic, physical hoardings found vent on social media. Throwing caution to the winds, the BJP online supporters posed serious governance questions to the Congress on projects that were not completed in the fifteen years, on promises that were never fulfilled from the last elections, on misappropriation of humongous public funds over time, and the like.[15]

The questions the Congress could bypass with the hoardings had to be faced directly on social media. For example, the non-implementation of the Assam Accord, the unfinished Bogibeel bridge for more than three decades, were failures of the government that the Assam electorate could relate to. It seemed that these questions and attacks broke the confidence of the Congress leadership. Online volunteers of the party could never save the leadership and match up to the facts that stared the Congress in the face. Rhetoric could never take away the merit of an argument. Slighted and broken, the Congress quickly changed its goalpost, much to the liking of the BJP.

The Congress's Communication Loses Steam

Since December end, the messages emerging from the Congress changed in focus, content and tone multiple times. At one point in time, the messages changed twice a week. The calm poise and confidence of an incumbent party transformed into a hazy frenzy. It seemed as if the Congress wanted to defend itself in many ways by saying multiple things at the same time but all without focus.

Some billboards announced the proof of progress in Assam like an award ceremony hailing Tarun Gogoi while some hoardings raised the issue of more than 210 'useless' meetings of Union ministers taking place in Assam since 2014. The state of confusion was so high that people could not decipher the mixed signals such a message sent.

Not only did the Congress express confusion in addressing what it wanted to communicate, it also managed to showcase a very elitist and ungrounded side of political campaigning. In one of the hoardings, glossy, young models spoke about growing intolerance in the state and advocated the right to freedom to eat whatever they wanted.

This communication seemed to have been borrowed from the beef controversy that had gripped Bihar during its assembly elections. But little research was done to find out if this issue affected the population in Assam at all and if other concerns were higher on priority for the electorates like unemployment, poverty, clean drinking water, infrastructure and corruption.

The result was that the public, which had begun by warming up to the trust card waved by the Congress party in the first part of the campaign, started feeling disconnected with and alienated from the party.

The Congress's Modi Card Volte Face

The subsequent failure of its campaign efforts made the Congress angry and caustic. Miffed by the responses of the public, the Congress began to caricature Modi. The idea was to shift the focus away from Tarun Gogoi and itself, and accuse the two and a half years of BJP rule at the Centre for everything wrong in the country and state. Additionally, it also demanded accountability from the central government.

Caricatures in a political campaign, splashed over billboards and hoardings, are a very new phenomenon in Indian electioneering. In fact, credit must go to the Congress for the fantastic usage of this art in this form. It opened up a new form of creative political communication via caricatures on big billboards, which was otherwise only relegated to newspapers and TV ads. No political party had attacked its opponents via cartoons and billboards during elections prior to this experiment in Assam. It was a leap from satire being used by the fourth pillar of Indian democracy to street satire being tried by political parties. The BJP was taken aback with this new, bold and interesting experiment, but there was a major loophole in the way it was utilized by the Congress.

The form and tone of a few caricatures went beyond the parameters of social and political decency. By reducing the image of the prime minister to scatological references on life-sized hoardings cheapened the level of political discourse. The unpalatable content and form of the communication exposed the vulnerability of a government that had not done much to talk about its achievements.

Such distasteful attacks suggested crises of thought leadership within the Congress camp. With lack of substantial issues to talk on, the Congress chose an abusive alibi implicating the prime minister. It exposed the complete lack of an agenda on the Congress's part. It also brought into open the shifty attitude of the Congress in its response to demands of accountability from the public for its fifteen years of administration in the state. By trying to focus the state's attention on Delhi and Modi, the Congress assumed that the BJP's narrative would crumble against the allegations. Attacking Modi was easy but to appeal to the public with a well-defined and articulated electoral agenda was a task that the Congress seemed reluctant to take on.

What the Congress did not account for, or miscalculated, was the general mood of the people and their awareness. When a seasoned politician like Tarun Gogoi dragged a national leader into day-to-day political bickering within the state, he falsely assumed the tirade against the prime minister would shift the public's focus away from state-level issues to national concerns.

Besides, the attack on Modi proved counterproductive for the Congress and began to become an advantage for the BJP. The people of Assam did not take well to the mockery that the Congress subjected the prime minister to. A state, which is known for its mildness in language and grace in speech, the name calling and cartoon caricatures of the highest office bearer of the country hurt the Assamese sensibilities. People found the concept low in taste and caustic in nature—not befitting the parliamentary grace with which elections are fought in India. They felt that with no checks and balances in place, the Congress had deteriorated the standard of public political debate in Assam.

A negative campaign from the ruling dispensation is seen as a diversionary tactic to tilt the focus away from its work. Elections are important milestones for the incumbent to share its report card with the people. The electorate expects to judge the government on the work done in public interest during its tenure. The Opposition, on the other hand, is expected to poke holes in the grand standing narrative set by the incumbent. However, in Assam, the incumbent very slyly focused its entire messaging on questioning the policies of the Union government in a state election. This carried the risk of being interpreted by the common people as an attack on their collective wisdom.

Peaking at the Right Time

A successful campaign ensures that close to the election day, public support for its party is at its peak. Besides, at the polling station, there should be one strong reason that reverberates in the minds of the voters and based on which he/she decides whom to vote for. Ram Madhav, the BJP in-charge for Assam elections, was particularly worried about the party campaign peaking at the right time. In an election campaign, the political issues to be raised should ideally be spaced out so that the momentum builds up steadily. The party which identifies itself closely with the advocacy of that one central theme generally emerges victorious.

The party began its communication by rolling out a set of hoardings that had important tribes and communities in Assam holding hands together. This communication was meant to dispel the myth that the BJP is a party of north Indians disconnected with the reality of Assam and one fiddling with the unity and integrity of the state's multicultural society. It asserted the BJP's resolve to work for all communities irrespective of communal, religious, tribal or ethnic identities towards a safe and developed Assam.

Thereafter, a scathing, negative campaign targeting Tarun Gogoi was launched. Inspired by the Congress's innovative use of satire, the BJP borrowed a catchphrase used by Gogoi. *'Baad diya hai'*, a phrase with no easy English translation, can loosely be interpreted as 'ignore it'. It was liberally used by Gogoi to evade any uncomfortable questions about his misgovernance. He seemed to have infamously and insensitively said 'Baad diya hai' in one of the interviews post floods in Assam invoking the references to foreign countries and how they also coped with floods. Insensitive comments and responses like these had become a part of the political folklore around Tarun Gogoi's rule and had, with time, degenerated into a topic of political jest. The BJP launched an ad campaign, hopeful of riding on the popularity of this catchphrase and as a response to the Congress's caricature of Modi. All the major billboards and hoardings in Assam had a laughing Mr Chief Minister oblivious to pathetic situations and facts depicted alongside his frame saying 'Baad diya hai'.[16] The tagline became incorporated in TV shows and satires on a daily basis. People on the streets began using this tagline freely to make fun of Tarun Gogoi and his rule.

Political communication has a twin-fold agenda. On the one hand, a political party interacts with the voters and on the other, it interacts with its supporters and karyakartas. Boosting the morale of the workers is as important as consolidating and propagating its central message among the public. When a party worker, who is fighting out lone battles on the streets, sees the party's aggressive posturing on the billboards, he feels enthused and hopeful. He starts to believe that his hard work in the grassroots will find a force multiplication from the party. This has a huge cascade effect and helps build an electoral wave.

While the Congress started its high-octane campaign around December 2015—a good four months prior to the election, the BJP waited till early February to begin its assault. For the initial two months, Congress posters were up in every street of Guwahati. The BJP's absence from the campaign space made its workers and supporters jittery. Holding on to the strategy of peaking at the right time in this wake of intense pressure from the party workers is not easy. And that it is where a campaign in-charge has to be persistent. The BJP held on to its cards firmly till February and then rolled out its intensive campaign during the last two months—so much so that every possible campaign space was monopolized by the party's message. Public memory is usually short. What the Congress said in December and January was forgotten by March and April.

Exploiting the Fear

During our campaign trail, an Uber cab driver in Guwahati expressed his insecurity with us: 'If BJP does not come to power this time, Assam will be the next Kashmir. Soon we will be a minority in our own land. Soon we will be forced to leave our ancestral land and seek refuge elsewhere. But where will we go? Who will give us jobs? How will we sustain ourselves?'[17] This threat against the changing ethnic demography of the state was palpable. The land and resource pressure created high levels of insecurity. A genuine sense of fear for an uncertain future should not be denigrated with a pejorative term like xenophobia. However vexed the political implication of this reality, this public sentiment could not be ignored.

Khilonjiya (indigenous) identity was a coinage that was drawn from the identity question that haunted every discussion we had with a layman on the street to the editors of respected newspapers to the political party members at the party office. The idea of becoming a minority in one's own land, the fear of cultural decimation, the palpable reality of the illegal occupation of land by Bangladeshis might sound like politically incorrect concerns, but were the topics of discussion at coffee and tea stalls across the state.

It was important to acknowledge the problem in the form it existed. It was important to accept that the form of address used by most common men and women might have been wrong, but the reason of this prevalent discontent among the masses was not an emotion to be dismissed lightly.

For any politician or political party or political movement, the primary objective at hand is to express and later address the issue plaguing millions of people they choose to represent. In such a situation, to not speak about an issue of such wide relevance might have passed a test of a closeted idea of theoretical political correctness but would have also exposed the disconnect from reality.

Using political correctness to evade the risk of raising and expressing a political reality has seeped so deeply into the political consciousness of our times that to raise issues like illegal migration of Muslims, for instance, becomes a communal rather than an economic and political question. Silence, which nurtures a soft vote bank based on selective ignorance of larger implications of those concerns, has created a cloak of impenetrability on issues of political significance, so much so that political parties more often than not choose to not talk about the issue at all.

The BJP leadership took a call to make this concern an electoral issue. But the leadership was also conscious of the fact that a state like Assam which identifies with its uniquely secular tradition of Azan Fakir, cannot afford to have any hint of communalism arising out of this purely political concern.

As discussed in earlier chapters, the facts were alarming. Between 2001 and 2011, the Muslim population in Assam had risen considerably. Six Muslim-dominated districts in Assam had increased to nine. Dhubri, Badruddin Ajmal's constituency had the largest Muslim population of 80 per cent. Barpeta showed the highest growth rate of Muslim population between the two census years—around 12 per cent. And most of these districts were border districts.

Looking at these figures was not a Hindu–Muslim concern but a concern of illegal migration from across the border. The fear of becoming an alien in one's own land was more to do with culture than religion. Wasbir Hussain, a renowned political commentator based out of Guwahati and also a consulting editor to national and local media houses, once shared in a conversation with us, 'There is no question of communalization in Assam. There is polarization and it is genuine. An Assamese Muslim man in Assam will prefer marrying an Assamese Hindu girl and vice versa than the Muslim man from Assam marrying a Bombay Muslim woman.'

Realizing the importance of the issue, the BJP launched an aggressive campaign on the issue of leadership. Rumours that Maulana Badruddin Ajmal might join hands with the Congress made matters clear for the electorate of Assam. Maulana, known for openly endorsing and nurturing migrants from Bangladesh had once asserted that he would be the kingmaker of Assam. Someone needed to voice these issues, and the BJP chose to be the one to bell the cat.

A few autorickshaws in Dibrugarh carried a poster that had Badruddin Ajmal on one side and Sarbananda Sonowal on the other, asking the people to choose the next chief minister between them. The poster represented the stark contrast between the khilonjiya and the 'other' identities to decide the leadership in Assam. Such messaging put forth a subtle polarization plank that hit the Assamese subconscious deeply.

BJP benefitted from shunning aside political correctness. The issue of illegal migration in Assam has been a much-debated issue since the elections in 1946. It is ironic and shameful for the political establishment in this country that between 1946 and 2016 nothing changed in the poll plank. No measures have addressed the issue that had been plaguing Assam since its very birth.

In order to effectively impact a state like Assam and ferret it out from the jaws of the Congress at an electoral point in time when the party has very little impressive ground presence, it was extremely important to understand and respect the pulse of the people. It was crucial for the BJP to make this election a citizens' campaign. Issues such as poverty, unemployment, violence against women, etc., are issues that people anywhere in this country relate to and immediately connect with. Elections are fought on these concerns every time, but elections are won on emotional pitches, which is exactly what the BJP managed to do.

Letting the Maulana Malign

As discussed earlier, siding openly with the Maulana would have meant political suicide for the Congress. Just in the previous assembly election in 2011, the Congress had invoked an aggressively pro-ethnic Assamese stand by asking the rhetorical question—'Who is Badruddin Ajmal?'—that had helped catapult the Congress to a landslide victory hitherto unseen in the history of Assamese politics. Departing from its fundamental position on an alliance with Ajmal seemed improbable.

Yet, five years is a very long time in politics. The projections and the electoral numbers suggested that Maulana and the Congress together would have given the alliance an invincible edge. Caught in this fix over the alliance, the responses of the Congress party on this question of political complication ranged from asserting in a press conference that they were confident of winning a majority alone to saying that they do would not mind a 'maha-understanding' of 'like-minded parties'. The Congress carefully kept itself one step away from openly seeking a *mahagathbandhan*-like alliance in Assam.

It is very interesting to observe how a party desperate to win Assam was responding to the calls of political alterations by the very minute. While the benefits of an 'all against the BJP' alliance were visible in the freshly concluded Bihar elections—something that rekindled the hope for the Congress in Assam—the possibility of a severe public backlash against the alliance made it a risky proposition. Therefore, the tightrope of this situation made the Congress susceptible to communication faux pas.

The BJP, on the other hand, tried every bit to exploit this situation to its advantage. It kept the gossip mill running around the possible coming together of the Congress and the AIUDF. The streets in the Brahmaputra valley were littered with pamphlets and posters saying '*Bujha bujhi hoi gol* [a secret deal has been done].' Calling this 'behind the curtain understanding' and a 'clandestine combine' to give Ajmal the throne of Dispur, the BJP laid bare the Congress's strategy. What it had planned to do secretly was now out in the public glare!

'Poribortan' in Assam

It was clear after a point in time, somewhere towards the end of March that a political wave was sweeping Assam. There was a demand for poriborton (change) in the state arising out of all quarters and corners. It also helped that even the media houses in Assam had started to popularize the term in its demands for poriborton against corruption, unemployment, misgovernance, lack of swift decision making, nepotism etc. on their discussion forums and public debates. In the last leg of the campaign of the BJP, the party wanted the theme of 'change' to be fixated in the minds of the people.

It is interesting to see how the word poriborton had become an avoided term for the BJP after the Bihar fiasco. The communication for poriborton had suffered a crushing defeat in Bihar and it was not a term one wanted to use at the outset for the Assam campaign, despite its aptness. However, there were distinct reasons why the theme failed to capture the mind space of voters in Bihar as it did so decisively in Assam.

In Bihar, it was not clear till the last moment of the electoral campaign cycle what the BJP was asking for poriborton against. Nitish Kumar's campaign team had successfully managed to script a narrative of '*Badh chala Bihar*' and '*Bihar mein bahaar ho, Nitish Kumar ho*', and the BJP's cry for poriborton felt like a misplaced and out-of-place slogan.

In Assam, in contrast, the BJP had successfully managed to take a leaf out of the Bihar campaign. It established first what was wrong with the incumbent ruling party. It then came closer to the electorate in defining together the fear of a possible election outcome in the event of a Bihar-like mahagathbandhan fanned and popularized by media speculations all the while. Finally, it demanded poriborton. The message was very clear and struck the right chord with the people.

The overall electoral blitzkrieg between the Congress and the BJP was won by the BJP also because the latter remained focused and repetitive on its core issue. As data from ground and focused conversations populated on to dashboard screens, every argument that was made in smaller brainstorming sessions made it to press briefings, TV debates, billboards, TV advertisements, radio jingles and big rallies. Messages were amplified via multiple channels of communication and spread and reverberated like a seismic wave across the state, right at the grassroots.

Tiding over Pressures

Despite this election turning into a wave election, there was a last attempt by the Congress to snatch back Assam from the jaws of the near successful BJP. And this attempt was far more dangerous to the democratic health of the state than any of its strategies adopted by far.

In a desperate attempt to turn the focus of the campaign, the Congress raised the issues of the 1985 killings, post-1996 violence and secret encounters in full-page newspaper advertisements. Assam, a state that had burned and suffered at the hands of several such unfortunate incidents of violence, had the potential to get rekindled at such gory reminders. But then at the altar of elections do political parties really care for such risks?

An electoral loss in Assam was something the Congress just couldn't afford. The Congress's campaign aggression did not limit itself to the state level issues. On the morning of 9 April, just two days before the second phase of the campaign, a full-page advertisement with the picture of Qutubuddin Ansari—the quintessential image of the 2002 Gujarat riots—appeared in all leading Assamese dailies.[18] The advertisement asked voters—'Does Modi's Gujarat always mean development? Do you want Assam to be Gujarat of this kind?'[19] Was the intent of the advertisement not obvious—to communalize and polarize the elections? Was the intent not to instil fear in the minds of the minorities of Lower Assam and swing them in its favour? It was the same Congress who only a few days back was preaching how Shankar–Azan unity was the essence of Assam. Did this rhetoric not have much value for their realpolitik now? Most people we interacted with to study the impact of this advertisement could not understand the import of the image of a crying man with folded hands juxtaposed with a message critical of Modi. An image that virtually became synonymous with Gujarat riots was largely unknown in this region of the country. The move further backfired on the Congress when Qutubuddin filed a complaint against the party for using his face without his permission in an attempt to impact poll outcomes.[20]

All these reactions to the Congress's last-mile endeavours to stop the BJP coming to power conveyed the outcome quite clearly by now. Later, the election results showed that even if the AIUDF and the Congress had come together for elections, joining hands, it could not have stalled the saffron juggernaut from claiming the seat of power in Dispur.

The Modi Magic

On 5 February 2016, Prime Minister Narendra Modi addressed a rally in Moran. Moran is a census town in the Dibrugarh district of Upper Assam and the constituency that elected Sarbananda Sonowal as its MLA in 2001. Dibrugarh University is also the place where Sarbananda Sonowal attended college and began his political journey.

Besides, Moran is a politically relevant place. It has a high concentration of people from the Moran tribe, which is where it draws its name from, as well as a sizeable Ahom population.

The Morans as a community have always asserted their identity as separate from many other tribes that inhabit Upper Assam. Though as Vaishnavites, their similarity to the Motoks is significant. While the Morans are classified as Ahoms, of late, they have been demanding a reserved status. Historical records reveal that the Morans were an indigenous community of Upper Assam. When Ahoms migrated to the areas, they married into the Morans in order to consolidate their reign in the region. But despite familial ties, the Morans and the Ahoms have shared a patchy relationship.

Tarun Gogoi hailed from the Ahom community. The historical paternalistic attitude of the Ahoms towards the other smaller communities, such as the Motoks, the Morans and the Sutiyas has been a cause of animosity between the communities. Tarun Gogoi had received almost uniform and unwavering support from the Ahoms by far. The Morans too had been kind to the Gogoi leadership. For the BJP, it was crucial to forge an alliance of smaller communities to challenge the Ahom vote base of the Congress.

Therefore, the choice of holding a rally in Moran was part of the larger agenda of reaching out to the community that traditionally has been voting for the Congress. It was also an informed decision considering that the support of most of the Assamese community was essential for scripting victory in the state. Moran was also chosen to appeal to the tea-growing community that majorly populates the constituency. Hence, historical and realpolitik reasons, all came together in BJP's decision. The public rally at Moran was to pay a much richer dividend in the later parts of the campaign process.

People from far flung villages gathered to listen to Modi. Some of them had travelled all the way on boats and walked for hours to come and see the prime minister. His helicopter landed to the drumbeats of various tribes who had come together to welcome him. The prime minister also joined in the drumbeating celebration later. Cultural programmes featuring unique dance and music forms of various local tribal groups had been organized.

Coming down heavily on the Tarun Gogoi–led Congress government in Assam, Modi reminded the people of the injustices done to them by the Congress. He recounted how he had inaugurated the gas cracker project at Dibrugarh after twenty-five years of its conceptualization by the Congress government at the Centre and in the state.

The gas cracker project was a part of the Assam Accord signed between the leaders of the Assam Movement and the Government of India in 1985. The prime minister reiterated how the leaders of the Congress had purposely kept the gas cracker plant bereft of action to milk it as a vote bank over the past five elections. The response of the crowd was maddening.

By invoking a reference to this historical negligence, Prime Minister Modi was successful in establishing that the Congress had never valued public opinion and aspirations and had always indulged itself in petty politics of power grabbing.

As compared with the Congress, he established his government and the BJP as an action-oriented group who in just two-and-a-half years of coming to power had settled the matter swiftly and inaugurated the plant. The message did not miss its mark. An election campaign which had by now successfully established the Congress's anti-incumbency saw in this rally the hope of much-needed change in Assam, emanating from the top leadership of the party. Later, Modi signed off by invoking, '*Agar aapke jeevan mein anand lana hai toh Assam mein Sarbananda lana hai* [If you wish to bring joy to your lives, bring Sarbananda to Assam].'

In the far hills and plains of the North-east, Modi occupies a near cult status. When Modi invoked the reference of his past as a tea seller, he catered to the community which had gathered to listen to him in huge numbers. The mere mention of the fact that he had been a chai wallah in his past profession drew him into the intimate coterie of the tea workers' community. Migrants, as most of them are, also identified with a leader who did not belong to Delhi but having migrated to Delhi from his hometown claimed the city as his own after gaining power. He gave them hope for change.

The rally in Moran was intended to make a dent in the Kuli support for the Congress. It is from here on in the campaign that the migrant labourers settled primarily in Upper Assam and working in tea gardens, broke away from the Congress fold.

Also, the Modi government had taken many initiatives that convinced the people of his fidelity to mass issues. In contrast to the Congress, which sent its Rajya Sabha MP from Assam, Dr Manmohan Singh, to Delhi as the prime minister, Modi in just a span of two years had shown immense commitment to the issues of the North-east.

For example, for the first time in the history of independent India, Barak valley—with a population double the size of Goa—was connected with a rail link directly to Delhi under the Modi government. On 21 November 2015, after a nearly two-decades-long negotiation with the central and state governments, for the first time, the Modi government opened up the broad gauge Silchar–Lumding rail line which benefitted not just Assam but also Tripura, Manipur and Mizoram.

Several such developmental initiatives have been long pending in the region. For instance, the Bogibeel bridge was proposed as part of the Assam Accord in 1985. It was supposed to be the longest bridge across the Brahmaputra connecting the north and south bank. The project had been languishing for over thirty years. The BJP used its government at the Centre to rapidly relaunch and complete some such projects. These were political moves to differentiate the BJP's alacrity in dealing with the development needs of Assam. It stood in sharp contrast to the Congress's colossal failure to finish several of its inaugurated projects.

Coupled with the charisma of Modi and the party's decision to go step by step towards uniting the larger Assamese society under one banner, the rally was a brilliant starting point of the electoral battle. With this beginning, the BJP found its narrative and energy to sustain the campaign over the next two aggressive months of political blitzkrieg. It seemed as if the drums that Modi beat on the side lines of the rally were symbolic of the victory drumbeats of the BJP to reverberate three months later.

chapter five

BATTLING THE WAR

'The genius of politics lies in the exploitation of fears and the invention of new ones.'

—Ajit Doval

~

The BJP started with very little in Assam. But the hard work of the RSS cadre over decades had prepared a fertile ideological ground for the BJP to electorally reap dividends. The rejuvenation of the party's prospects after the switchover of key Congressman, Himanta Biswa Sarma, had further strengthened BJP's position. The enthusiasm of the party cadre in keeping alive the flame of anti-incumbency against the Congress government had created an atmosphere that demanded change. Coupled with all this, the metaphorical war cries to fight the Last Battle of Saraighat this election had echoed in the basic Assamese political conscience.

The Last Battle of Saraighat: Phase 1

In 1671, the Ahom kingdom fought a bitter battle under the leadership of Ahom general Lachit Borphukan, against the Mughals. Through diplomacy, tact and strategic planning, Lachit Borphukan was able to defeat the Mughal forces and restore the Ahom pride.

The Battle of Saraighat has always carried huge symbolic value in the hearts and minds of the Assamese. The valour of Lachit is evoked every time there is a threat to the jaati–maati–bheti (nation, land, home) of the Assamese. The Assam Movement was fought with the same vigour and drew its inspiration from the Battle of Saraighat. The movement compared the Bangladeshi-migrant-led attack on the Assamese culture and society with the Mughal attack on the Ahom nation. The leaders of the movement took an oath in the name of Lachit Borphukan to oust these illegal migrants.

This historic battle was recounted in the 2016 electoral battle. So much so that the entire election was branded as *'Saraighator Xheikh Ron'*, or 'the Last Battle of Saraighat'. In one of his public interactions, Sarbananda Sonowal called this election the Last Battle of Saraighat. It is from here that the campaign found its unifying voice. In the light of so many disparate issues that needed a binding force, this historical allegory was the one that had the immense potential to bind the entire campaign together.

The cry to protect the independent identity of Assam, the appeal to unite against external aggression by cultural contaminators, the emotive pitch of political and cultural unity despite economic disparity and inequality was what made the BJP term the 2016 election as the Last Battle of Saraighat.

Assam went to polls on 4 April and 11 April. The state observed massive polling percentages to the tune of 85 per cent. Such voter turnout was unprecedented in Assam. Enthusiasm and fear—two disjointed emotions, had gripped the electorate. General enthusiasm was mainly driven by the hope to finally see poriborton after fifteen years of the Congress regime. However, more importantly, voters thronged at the polling booths as if it was their last chance to save the Axomiya Jaati. Political commentators compared the massive turnout to the days of the 1985 assembly elections that were held in the midst of the popular Assam Movement. For the past three decades, ever since the 1985 elections, no one had observed such frenzy at the polling booths.

The way the Assamese voters indicated their reason for the vote in our surveys hinted at the first signs of a wave election in the state. With each passing day and each election rally, more and more voters joined the war cry of the Last Battle of Saraighat. While early on in the campaign issues like development and jobs seemed to matter the most, closer to the polling dates all these issues seemed to have folded around the core issue of identity and security. Our internal surveys started showing a massive 50 per cent respondents choosing 'illegal immigrants' as the most important issue in the election. When voters so decisively chose a single predominant issue for an election—it could be safely assumed that the elections were headed for a showdown or a referendum. All that the BJP had to do was to sharpen the focus of the electorate on this single discernible issue of illegal migrants, claim itself as a saviour of the Axomiya Jaati and ensure it won the referendum.

A week prior to the first phase of polling, the wave seemed to have strengthened. The media stringers, who usually interview voters for opinion polls of various media agencies, shared interesting anecdotes of how the support for the BJP was speedily building up. The state bureaucracy, which was initially using its raw power to tear down any BJP poster or flags they could lay their hands on, suddenly began to have a change of heart. Not only could they sense the changing mood of people, but they also wanted to be on the 'right' side of the political 'change'. The local level police functionaries gradually adopted a more neutral posture.

An important litmus test for a politician to gauge the changing electoral winds is to observe the way the village and block level officials share their token 'gifts'. For the longest time this exchange of pleasantries had virtually dried up at the BJP district offices. The tide decisively shifted only around the third week of March when these local body officials started queuing up at the offices and houses of BJP district and mandal presidents and the local BJP candidates to offer their 'gifts' to the party.

Phase 1 of the polls was to be held in Upper Assam (the eastern part), the Barak valley (the Bengali-speaking southern part) and the North Cachar hill areas that included Dima Hasao and Karbi Anglong. Each of these regions had their own share of electoral distinctiveness and required micro strategies for electoral battles.

While Sarbananda Sonowal steadfastly focused on securing his tricky constituency of Majuli, a riverine island, Himanta

Biswa supported him by freeing him up from the worries of other constituencies. The whirlpool rallies of Himanta Biswa in the run-up to the last days of the campaign sealed the fate for BJP. His schedule used to be packed with seven to eight political rallies per day, divided by intermittent strategy sessions and ending with one-on-one meetings with supporters from his constituency.

Surprisingly, the AGP cadre worked overtime to garner support for their alliance partner, the BJP, at times working even harder than their BJP counterparts. Interestingly, quite a few young ethnic Assamese Muslim voters subscribed to this war cry and were found voting for the BJP. Although the statistical significance was minimal, it is just another indication of a strong political wave which sometimes even takes the Opposition vote along the way through the sheer strength of perception.

Intellectual 'Fatwa'

Assam was about to go to the first phase of polls on 4 April 2016. One day ahead of the polls, about forty people led by an eminent intellectual and a former professor of Gauhati University, Hiren Gohain, signed a petition and called a press conference asking the people of the state to not vote for the BJP. The petition mentioned that BJP was trying to divide the state on various communal lines and it was 'the biggest enemy of the state'. The tone and tenor of directing the electorate to not vote for a specific political party was nothing less than issuing a fatwa.[1] Asking people not to vote for a specific party using the influence of their offices and social standing is tantamount to intentionally subverting the democratic process. This even goes against the basic principles of natural justice. It was a plot to hold the press conference right on the eve of the election, so that with the model code in effect, the BJP was in no position to respond to the charges made against it.

This created a major storm in Assam. As a quick response, another group of intellectuals led by former Gauhati University vice chancellor, Nirmal Kumar Choudhury, and former Assam director general of police, Nishinath Changkakoti, signed a counter petition questioning the motive of the likes of Hiren Gohain. The petition termed the appeal by Hiren Gohain and group as anti-democratic. It lambasted these intellectual elites of Assam for taking the liberty of leading the public opinion of Assam against a political party and posing a threat to free and fair elections.

It is an extremely worrying trend in Indian democracy these days where the self-styled ideologically motivated individuals, camouflaged as 'intellectuals' of the country, on various occasions have led the public opinion to satisfy their partisan goals.

It is saddening that the moral high ground they try to take just by being what they are, is often misleading and not grounded in reality. Often it is infuriating because the plane from where they speak is a sacred plane of reverential authority that Indian society seeped in a unique cultural tradition bestows on teachers, academics and intellectual minds. It is infuriating because this position of social reverence has been misappropriated and manhandled by these intellectuals to serve a syndicate they have formed with one of the most influential groups or institutions across the globe. Not always, but some of the times, their outrage, intentionally or unintentionally, serves a political purpose. For instance, highly acclaimed Kannada writer Dr U.R. Ananthamurthy went on record to state that he will not live in India with Narendra Modi as the prime minister.[2] This served as a triggering point to build a political campaign against Narendra Modi by vested political interest groups. Ananthamurthy allowed his respectable social standing to be used as a political tool. Moreover, he did not deem it fit to even disclose to the public that in 2004 he had sought a ticket from the Congress to fight the parliamentary elections from the Bangalore south seat.[3]

The Last Battle of Saraighat: Phase 2

The Phase 2 of the polls were scheduled for 11 April in the central and the western parts of the Brahmaputra valley along with the Bodoland region. The ruling Congress party headed by Tarun Gogoi began to realize the depth of the public anger after the first round of polling on 4 April. It was expected that the Phase 2 polls would be an even more bitter triangular contest between the BJP-led alliance, the Congress and the AIUDF. This phase included places in the Lower Assam region with a high concentration of Bangladeshi immigrants. Over thirty seats that went to poll in the second round had more than 40 per cent Muslim presence. These constituencies were up for grabs for the Congress or the AIUDF. The BJP focused its attention on the other thirty seats.

The Congress unleashed a massive polarization campaign against the BJP in the minority dominated areas. Congress workers started spreading the rumours of how the Gujarat 2002 massacre would be repeated in the state if the minorities did not vote for Gogoi. In fact, many Bangla-speaking clerics also tried to preach that a vote for the AIUDF would be an indirect vote for the BJP. The Congress had realized that almost all segments of non-Muslim Assamese voters were deserting it and the only way to make a comeback was to try and garner the minority votes. Badruddin Ajmal too had sensed the Congress game plan and was seen working overtime to protect his turf.

On the other hand, the BJP's problem in this highly polarized phase was its inherent weakness in the Lower Assam region. The BJP as a party had for long been a minor player in Assam and lacked a cadre of its own in most parts of the state. In Phase 2, the BJP's cadre was supplemented by nearly 20,000 workers of the RSS and other affiliated organizations like the Lok Jagran Manch. The RSS also utilized the network of Ekal Vidyalay teachers, who have a very good influence among the local populace, especially in the Bodo areas on the north bank.

The booth-level infrastructure of the AGP was a big game changer. In fact, the alliance with the much-depleted the AGP, which was originally frowned upon by many BJP local leaders, proved to be a boon in a highly polarized Phase 2. The recent shift of many Congress leaders to the BJP, especially the master strategist, Himanta Biswa Sarma, also helped the party in nullifying the Congress game plan in many of these seats.

The Axomiya wave was at its peak during Phase 2 of the polls. Minorities wanted to stop the BJP's chances of forming the government in Dispur. Minorities were worried that Ajmal, with massive business interests outside the state and in the Gulf, may not want to provoke the BJP-led central government in Delhi. So, the Congress, as a national party, could be more useful for them at the moment to counter BJP's rise. There were sporadic reports that some of the AIUDF voters in Lower Assam were going back to the Congress. The strategic shift of the minority votes to the Congress worried not just the AIUDF but also the BJP. Any consolidation in minority votes towards the Congress would significantly damage the BJP's chances. If Muslims had decided after Friday prayers during the week of second round of polling to vote strategically for the Congress, it could have put a brake on the BJP juggernaut.

The Last Touch

Himanta Biswa Sarma planned more than 200 rallies in the state in a short span of a month or a little more. Sarma travelled from one end of Assam to the other, raising issues of unemployment, poverty, illegal migration, corruption and dynasty politics and made these few the battle cry that Assam needed to be saved from. Besides, his speeches infused with gusto and energy swayed the opinions of the youth and convinced the others about the issue of Assamese identity. Wherever he went, there was a charismatic wave that followed his rally.

The last political rally was hosted by Himanta Biswa Sarma in his own constituency. Loved and adored as he is in his own constituency, Himanta could not find enough time to visit it during the campaign. But the goodwill for him in the constituency was such that on the last day of the campaign when he visited Jalukbari, it seemed as if the entire constituency had turned out to welcome him. Himanta delivered a very emotional speech and broke down on stage while saying that when he dies, Jalukbari should be the place where he must be cremated.

Women broke down, men looked shaken and moved, the youth raised the sky rending slogans and it was apparent that not just Jalukbari but the entire state would vote en masse for the BJP.

'It's a BJP wave. We have registered a historic win. I thank the people of Jalukbari,' Himanta tweeted soon after the result was declared on the morning of 19 May 2016.

Post-Election Analyses

In one of the most flattering analysis of BJP's campaign efforts in Assam, a noted psephologist Dr Praveen Patil remarked, 'We do indeed believe that after the 2014 elections this is the first time that the BJP has shown real creativity in tackling an adversary, for the BJP was in danger of becoming a one-point-strategy party of holding large Modi rallies and simply hoping for magic in polling booths after that. The result is telling. For the first time after 2014, BJP has achieved another Hindu vote spectrum in Assam, albeit this time not by building caste coalitions but by building ethnic and tribal partnerships.'[4]

While analysing the results, Ram Madhav shared his insight, 'A small mistake during the time of the polls can cost you the entire election. Luckily, in Assam, the BJP committed no mistake in its strategy. On the other hand, the Congress was on a slippery slope and it kept slipping.'

The BJP used the initial momentum it had after the 2014 Modi victory to build a robust on-ground network of volunteers and maintained a sharp and creative messaging that never let the Congress set any election agenda. The team of central and state leaders worked in tandem under the overall guidance of Prime Minister Modi and BJP president Amit Shah.

For the BJP, it was a complete sweep, a stupendous victory. The NDA combine won eighty-seven seats among the 126 assembly constituencies—winning virtually all the seats the alliance seriously contested in—keeping in mind that more than thirty-three seats had massive Muslim populations in the range of 60–95 per cent.

When the initial reports came in, favouring the BJP, the workers at the party headquarters at Hengrabari Road in Guwahati were jubilant. A party worker said, 'We stockpiled sweets and *gulal* last night itself as we were confident of our victory.' The winning beats on the *dhak*s and dholaks enticed every small and big leader to dance their hearts out.

The power had decisively shifted from the Rajiv Bhawan to Atal Bihari Vajpayee Bhawan. BJP had broken the North-eastern wall.

Ajmal Stunned

In a big embarrassment, the self-proclaimed kingmaker, Maulana Badruddin Ajmal, lost his own seat of South Salamara to arch-rival Wazed Ali Choudhury of the Congress by over 14,000 votes. Ajmal sang the following song to the *Telegraph* during an interview[5] on the evening of the result declaration: '*Hum bhari duniya mein tanha rah gaye, dil ke armaan aansuon mein bah gaye* [I have been left alone in this world, my dreams have been washed away in tears].'

On the eve of the voting, Ajmal had made an assertion—that the AIUDF would win nothing less than forty seats and neither the BJP nor the Congress could form the government without his support. When the bells tolled on the morning of vote counting, it dashed the dreams of the man who had fancied himself as the kingmaker. The AIUDF's tally also dipped to thirteen seats from eighteen in the 2011 assembly elections.

Ajmal's followers attributed their chief's defeat to counter polarization of Muslim votes in favour of the Congress instead of the AIUDF. Muslims, according to Ajmal,[6] were wary of the BJP's growing strength especially after its perceived wave in the first phase of the polling. They felt that this time the Congress was better placed to stop the BJP juggernaut. This shifting of loyalty of Muslim voters to the Congress in the minority-dominated areas of Lower Assam cost the AIUDF dearly.

However, there is another perspective to analyse Ajmal's defeat. Ajmal had hardly spent time among its core constituents and was busy managing his business interests globally. He spent most of his time away from the state and did not pay attention to the people's problems as an MP. As an ex-AIUDF MLA, Monowar Hussain, laments, 'Ajmal uses politics to expand his business. His main agenda is to earn more money.' In spite of the all-pervasive work done by his NGO Markazul Ma'arif, his long absence from the political scene of the state adversely impacted his clout in the Muslim-dominated regions of Lower Assam.

Ajmal had tried his best to reach out to the Congress for a pre-poll alliance. 'The AICC was also keen on a tie-up. So were Bihar chief minister Nitish Kumar and poll strategist Prashant Kishor,' Ajmal said.[7] However, it was the APCC that ruled out any possible alliance with Ajmal. Many believed that it was Ajmal's vaulting ambition and aggressive posturing as a kingmaker in state politics that irked the Congress, especially Gogoi. The Maulana often claimed that he would call the shots in case Assam had a hung assembly.

Post the election, Ajmal blamed the failure of the Congress and the AIUDF to reach to an understanding that cost both of them the election. A common belief among the political analysts was that lack of a mahagathbandhan of sorts in Assam spelled doom for the Congress and the AIUDF. The alliance could have consolidated the Muslim vote base and handed victory to the alliance.

However, with a hindsight benefit, a simple mathematical analysis shows how a near complete Hindu consolidation in favour of the BJP had already taken place. Had there been an alliance between the Congress and the AIUDF, and a 100 per cent vote transfer between the alliance partners, the BJP-led alliance would still have won more than seventy seats and the Congress–AIUDF combine couldn't have managed more than fifty-five seats.

This assessment shows how the 'united spectrum of Hindu votes' in Assam was formidable and reached an unprecedented scale, so much so that a Muslim consolidation could not have dented it. Such a pattern of voting has never before been observed in the electoral history of Assam. Even in the 1985 elections, which followed the famous Assam Movement, the polarization of the electorate in favour of one political formation was not so dramatic.

The Congress's Heartbreak

The elections results were earth-shattering for the Congress. It fell to its lowest tally of twenty-six seats in the history of state elections. Ten out of the fifteen sitting ministers of the Tarun Gogoi cabinet and several other Congress heavyweights and their close relatives who contested elections lost the battle of democracy in Assam. As a Congress leader correctly pointed out, 'When the wave hits, everything is washed away.'[8] Barring four ministers—Rakibul Hussain, Ajanta Neog, Nazrul Islam and Sukur Ali—all other ministers in the Gogoi cabinet lost the polls.

Several family members of long-term MPs and MLAs of the Congress also contested the elections. For instance, one senior minister, Bhumidar Barman, did not contest and vacated his Barkhetri assembly seat for his son, Diganta Barman, who also lost the seat. Angkita Dutta, daughter of APCC president, Anjan Dutta, who contested from Amguri in Sivasagar district in place of her father, also faced a similar fate. In Digboi, Rameswar Dhanowar, MLA since 1978, ensured the constituency was passed on to one of his sons, Gautam, but couldn't ensure his win. In Teok, the Congress replaced veteran MLA Membor Gogoi with his daughter-in-law, Pallabi Saikia Gogoi, who also lost. The practice of treating constituencies as a family fiefdom was a major campaign issue for the BJP. Himanta Biswa Sarma taunted the Congress party by calling it 'Ghar–Sansaar', after a popular Assamese TV show built around the story of a family.

The Congress was shocked by its defeat in Barak valley as all its four ministers from the region—Gautam Roy, Ajit Singh, Siddeque Ahmed and Girindra Mallick—lost their elections. Gautam Roy, a six-time legislature, and his son, Rahul Roy, were both nominated for the adjoining seats of Katlicherra and Algapur. Both lost their seats to the AIUDF. In Silchar, Lok Sabha MP Sushmita Deb's mother, Bithika Deb, was nominated for a Silchar seat after a gap of ten years. Bithika had won the Silchar seat in 2006 and relinquished it in 2011 for her daughter Sushmita. In 2014, Sushmita won the Lok Sabha seat from the same region. After Sushmita became an MP and gave up the assembly seat, the BJP's Dilip Paul won the by-election.

In 2016, Dilip retained the Silchar seat by defeating Bithika. While in the 2011 assembly polls, the BJP had failed to win any seat in Barak valley, this time it won nine of the fifteen seats in the region.

Upper Assam also saw a similar BJP sweep. The BJP created history by winning all seven seats in Dibrugarh district. Veteran Congress leaders—including former Union minister Paban Singh Ghatowar, former Assam minister Prithibi Majhi, three-time cabinet minister Pradyut Bordoloi, education minister Sarat Barkataky who was an MLA for twenty-five years—were defeated by the young and new faces of the BJP.

Then chief Minister Tarun Gogoi barely succeeded in protecting his fortress, Titabor. He defeated BJP's Kamakhya Prasad Tasa, the sitting Jorhat Lok Sabha MP, with a much lower victory margin. As the strongest bastions of the Congress fell, the mood in the Congress headquarters, Rajiv Bhawan in Guwahati, turned sombre. The party workers and supporters grieved at the way their party had been routed across Assam.

The End of the AGP's Exile

The assembly elections of 2016 ended the AGP's fifteen-year-long political exile from the state. While the AGP had ten sitting MLAs in the outgoing assembly, it managed to win fourteen seats in alliance with the BJP. What appears to be a modest gain for the AGP in numbers in fact was a big win for the party. In 2011, the AGP had contested 104 seats and won a paltry ten seats. In the 2016 elections, the AGP contested twenty-four seats in alliance with the BJP–BPF–AGP formation and six more seats in a 'friendly contest' with the BJP. Out of these thirty seats, the AGP achieved a handsome tally of fourteen seats. It was a big feat for a party that was depleted of resources and cadre base. In spite of the big gains, the AGP had made in alliance with the BJP, its existential questions still loom large.

Getting the AGP on board was a hotly debated issue for the BJP internally. Many within the BJP felt that siding with the AGP meant putting the regional party on an oxygen ventilator and resurrecting a dead force. But the numbers that emerged over data analytics reflected the benefit of partnering with the party. The alliance was predicted to yield big electoral gains for both the BJP and the AGP. However, stitching together this alliance was a difficult task.

The AGP's two-time chief minister Prafulla Kumar Mahanta–led faction was never convinced about the alliance largely because there was hardly any personal gain for him in the BJP-led government. On the other hand, the AGP president Atul Bora–led faction, which had not tasted power yet, was eager to jump sides and partner with the BJP. Even after the alliance was formally announced, Mahanta continued to create confusion in the BJP camp. He said that 'Sarbananda Sonowal was the BJP's chief ministerial candidate and not that of the alliance',[9] triggering speculation about the very sustainability of the alliance. However, it took much convincing and heavy negotiations before the rainbow alliance could be stitched and the ground prepared for the magic to unfold. The alliance triggered huge resentment among party members, resulting in resignations by some of them from the party and a few contesting the election as independent candidates.

More than the AGP leaders, it was the party workers that were enthused about the idea of an alliance with the BJP. They worked overtime to ensure that the AGP vote was transferred to the BJP. The enthusiasm was not matched in proportion by the BJP workers who still believed that the BJP could have reached the magic number on its own.

The BPF's Honeymoon Continues

The BPF repeated its achievement of the last assembly elections by winning all the twelve constituencies within the Bodoland Territorial Areas District (BTAD). It was possibly the biggest beneficiary of the alliance with the BJP. It smoothly sailed through the high anti-incumbency that had built up against the BPF when it was in alliance with the Congress. Closer to the assembly elections, BPF chief Hagrama Mohilary decided to withdraw support from the Congress-led government and sit in the Opposition. Hagrama's political gamble paid off really well.

A jubilant BPF chief Hagrama Mohilary gave credit to the people of the BTAD for the win. He said, 'It signifies that the people have faith in the BPF. It is the win of the people. We (BJP–AGP–BPF alliance) were confident of winning majority of the seats and form the next government in Dispur. The results were as expected.'[10]

Sonowal's Majuli

Majuli, one of the largest river islands in the world, located in the Brahmaputra, is also referred to as Assam's spiritual nerve-centre because of the presence of numerous satras (Vaishnavite monasteries) subscribing to the teachings of sixteenth-century

saint-reformer Srimanta Sankardeva. Majuli had been in news
due to its rapid erosion which has shrunk in size from 1200 sq.
km to 540 sq. km. However, Majuli as an assembly constituency
has hardly made news. It was never a VIP constituency until
the 2016 election when the BJP announced that its chief
ministerial candidate, Sarbananda Sonowal, would contest
from Majuli. The constituency has an electorate of 1,14,000,
of whom 43,000 belong to the Mishing tribe. The constituency
has invariably had a Mishing representative. Rajib Lochan Pegu,
the water resource minister and Congress candidate seeking
re-election, belonged to this tribe unlike rival Sonowal, who
was a Sonowal Kachari tribal from Dibrugarh district further
east. The demographic alignment had the potential to throw a
surprise for the BJP. If the Mishing votes weren't split, it could
be a significant problem for Sonowal. The Gana Shakti Party—
the small regional party that controls the Mishing Autonomous
Council—came to Sonowal's rescue. It fielded Ranjit Doley, also
a Mishing, from Majuli as an independent candidate, severely
denting the unity of the Mishing electorate. The *satradhikar*s
(monastery abbots)were brought in from Jorhat, to mobilize
the 71,000 non-tribal voters in favour of Sonowal.

As it became evident that the BJP's chief ministerial
candidate, Sarbananda Sonowal, was going to win from the
Majuli seat, the 'island of sorrow', Majuli, was joyful. A
couple of thousand people gathered at the subdivisional office
where the counting was held and celebrated when they heard
the results. In Sonowal's victory, they saw their long-cherished
dream take shape.

The worried Sonowal was offering puja at the Shiv Mandir
at Garmurh Chariali when the good news reached him. He

could finally breathe a deep sigh of relief. 'This is a blessing received from the people of Assam. It is a united effort by our alliance and the people of Assam accepted us. I will also thank the BJP leadership and especially the prime minister for a strong leadership which convinced the people of the state,' he said,[11] addressing the people before leaving for Guwahati where an even bigger celebration awaited him.

'Sowing saffron, reaping lotus'[12]

This interesting headline appeared in an article in the *Telegraph,* analysing the political reasons behind BJP's stupendous victory in the elections. The article lauded the political craft of the RSS in laying and nurturing the bedrock that allowed the BJP to grow in the state. A robust network of more than 800 shakhas in Assam helped create a new political space for the BJP and increased its acceptability among the electorates. In the words of Shekhar Gupta, 'The RSS can now enjoy its first, self-made political victory. Win or lose, the BJP is Assam's front-runner, from being non-existent three decades ago except for thousands of committed RSS workers, pracharaks and strategists brought in from all over. How they sowed the first seeds of their ideology, co-opted the massively popular Assam movement, converted its ethnic–chauvinistic impulse into an anti-Muslim one, built a launch pad for the BJP and then conjured up a local leadership is the stuff of political folklore.'[13]

It was indeed the hard work of generations of RSS ideological foot soldiers, that the BJP was going to form its first government in the state.

However, the work has just begun for the RSS in the region. Assam's victory opens up opportunities in other North-eastern states. It will work with renewed zeal in these states to capitalize on the BJP wave that has started from Assam. As hundreds of newly minted MLAs and other BJP leaders throng at the doors of the RSS *karyalay* (office), the Sangh has roles cut out for each of them. Each of them have been tasked to spread the good work done by the Modi-led central government and to build on the nationalistic fervour in their regions.

So Near, Yet So Far

There is a common belief in the political circles in Assam that whosoever becomes the education minister of the state, is doomed never to become the chief minister. Himanta Biswa Sarma was the outgoing education minister in Gogoi's cabinet and he missed out on being the chief minister of the new BJP-led government in Assam.

Being a perennial number 2 in the political edifice can be frustrating for anyone. Sarma, though dejected, kept up a bold, confident and smiling face. In the balance of power, Sarma was made the convener of a new formation—the NEDA to coordinate the political affairs of the entire North-east for the BJP. He was offered portfolios of his choice in the government and ended up with nine departments, including finance, health, Guwahati development department. He also retained the supposedly ill-fated education department. He is undoubtedly the strongest minister in the state with a clout that matches that of Chief Minister Sarbananda Sonowal.

But was Sarma's fight with Tarun Gogoi and the Congress leadership worth all the effort? Wouldn't he have been the natural choice as the next chief minister after Gogoi? Life had indeed come a full circle for Himanta-da, as he is popularly called by his supporters.

He candidly responds to these questions, 'In the middle of the election campaign, I got multiple feelers from Priyanka Gandhi to bring me back into the Congress fold. I was also offered the Congress Legislative Party leader position which would have meant the CM [chief minister] post had the Congress won the election. However, for me the Congress ship has passed and I do not regret the decision.'

He further adds that this election was no ordinary election. With a rapidly changing demography of the state—this is perhaps the last time the BJP could win the election with a decisive mandate. In 2021, according to Sarma, the ground reality would have changed so much that Ajmal would actually be the kingmaker and no party could ever form a government without his *dua* (blessings). No one knows whether Ajmal will politically survive the electoral defeat of 2016 and be ready for an even bigger battle in 2021. But one thing is certain, Himanta Biswa Sarma's steep ascendancy in political power hierarchy would keep Assamese politics ever fascinating.

chapter six

ELECTIONS AND INDIAN DEMOCRACY

'In the dance of democracy, people have been and will always be the kingmakers.'

~

In popular imagination, electoral victories in North-east India are attributed to those who govern at the Centre. Analysts argue that owing to the dependence of the North-east states on the central corpus of funds, they end up choosing the governing power in Delhi in order to ease out disbursement of finance. However, this opportunistic painting of the North-east purely on the basis of economic dependence completely reduces the relationship between the North-east with the rest of India to a transactional kind. It is true, but only partly so.

National versus Local

The national political parties, in general, have had a very hands-off approach to dealing with the North-east. As long as there has been a relative calm in the region, the North-east never figured in the agenda of the leadership in Delhi. In fact, the Congress party exemplified this approach in its more than fifty years of rule in the states of the North-east. We have earlier described how a transactional relationship thrived between the regional satraps and the Congress in Delhi. This was mutually beneficial and there was never a need to mainstream the issues of the North-east. It was far easier to label the region as 'marginalized' than discuss and deliberate on core issues of governance, human rights violations, corruption and ethnic concerns.

The North-east has enjoyed a unique politics of its own. Tribal, community and clan bonds had dominated any other discourse, including ideological, by far. Regional concerns and community allegiances rather than national agendas had stirred emotions and passions and decided electoral mandates for most of the electoral battles.

However, the fulcrum has shifted in the past few decades. With connectivity with the rest of India becoming easier and better, thanks to the digital and media explosion, governance and its competitive parameters have begun to inform political decision-making in the region. Besides, universal issues like infrastructure, ease of accessing government services, and health care are national concerns which have as much bearing on the local and regional issues as on the national platforms.

It is not just the cultural and linguistic diversity in the North-east that is striking, but also the sheer complexity of issues in different areas, often antagonistic to each other, that offer a unique strategic and intellectual challenge in order to develop a comprehensive understanding of the region. It is quite possible that people visiting each of these distinct parts will paint the region in their own colour and that the individual portraits might not coalesce with each other at all. Also, the definition and answer of 'How is the North-east?' will vary quite a lot from each other and that each one of them would be correct in their own versions.

Unfortunately, a comprehensive narrative, which explains the North-east as it is—in all its complexities—had been missing in the national imagination of India. Therefore, a well-run election campaign can contain the ingredients for the integration of the region with the rest of India. A good campaign can stitch national and regional consciousness around the ordinary concerns of the common man.

When Jharkhand chief minister Raghubar Das visited the tea plantation workers in Assam during the election campaign, there was a feeling of togetherness in identifying with the issues of general concern between Jharkhand and Assam. Similarly, when Jual Oram, the minister for tribal affairs, spoke to the Bodos of Assam during the campaign, there was a sense of empathy in trying to understand the tribulations of a fellow tribal community in Assam by a tribal minister from Odisha. Though just examples, but the interesting aspect of the election campaign in 2016 by the BJP was to narrate a familiar, national story that the common people in the state could relate to and identify with.

In spite of this, the gap between the national and the local was so huge that it was difficult to ignore the historical baggage and move on.

A United Assam in 2016

The British always looked at Assam as a buffer state. The British interest in Assam was limited to geographically securing its rule in

India from the other aggressors like the Chinese and the Japanese. A commercially viable tea cultivation model was used as a bait to interest the British gentlemen for serving in this part of the country. Till today, the streets of London remind us of the commercial buffer zone the British created in Assam every time one stumbles across tea shops with the aroma and tea leaves of Assam.

As if learning its rope from the British, the Congress too created a buffer zone in Assam. This zone has been a political buffer. As long as the local leaders delivered the state to the Congress party in elections, there was not much need to politically and nationally invest in the region. As long as the transaction sustained, it was all right to leave the state as it was, with all its faults and complaints, so as to maintain the power equilibrium. Therefore, Assamese concerns were seen as different from Indian concerns. Somehow the impression had been that the complexities of the state did not allow enough room for common grounds with the rest of India.

Throughout these years, the Congress had mastered Ali–Kuli–Bengali politics. For the Congress, electoral wins happened—year after year—with the en masse 60 per cent Ali–Kuli–Bengali vote bank. They never bothered with forging a larger unity of Assamese society or rebuilding the national discourse in the alienated part or addressing key issues of developmental concerns. This vote-bank based electoral laziness further alienated Assam from the rest of the country.

Even the highly popular Assam Movement, which was led by the upper-caste Assamese, could not bring diverse groups of the Assamese within its fold. Unifying Assam's Brahmaputra and the Barak valley remains a distant dream.

However, 2016 was different. The BJP stitched together an unprecedented social alliance offering a common platform to the Assamese, the Bengalis, tea garden labourers, the Adivasis, the Nepalis, the Hindi-speaking and the indigenous Muslims. It is this 'dream alliance' Ram Madhav referred to in his various press conferences.

The issue of illegal migration from Bangladesh that had become a civilizational question in the 2016 Assam assembly elections, further strengthened the ties of the question of national integrity and cultural pride. Much prior to the elections, our survey sheets clearly demonstrated that Assamese voices, in unison, were gearing up for a battle to save Axomiya Jaati. Sarbananda Sonowal's declaration of the elections as the Last Battle of Saraighat further turned on the emotional temperature of the polls. With a careful stitching of a narrative that pitted a young AASU activist in Sonowal against a potential *miya* (Bangladeshi Muslim) leader in Badruddin Ajmal, the voters in Assam were united across the spectrum. Some other surveys[1] revealed how tribal communities, Ahoms (otherwise antagonistic to BJP), backward communities and Dalits, and Assamese Muslims—all came together in this electoral battle to oust the Congress government from the seat of power.

These decisions to culturally interpret issues of regional concern, like that of migration, were not taken in a day. From connecting local issues to national ones, Assam gradually reintegrated with the national discourse. In 2016, it rightfully demanded its legitimate share for swift and equitable development. Impatient and passionate aspirations of the youth aggressively questioned the status quo and rejected those who failed to provide dignified employment opportunities. General citizens demanded a decent standard of living, health, education and equal opportunities of growth beyond the Ali–Kuli–Bengali placation of policy plans.

This seemingly electoral—but indeed a political and ideological—success in Assam has been scripted by a vote for change in the state. It is a vote shunning the political laziness of cherry-picked constituency victories to win elections towards a more cohesive and collective will of the people. It is an assertive people's mandate that has brought together the cultural–nationalist narrative of '*akhand sanskritik* parampara' (integrated cultural tradition) propounded by the RSS and the political narrative of cohesive nationalism of the BJP.

In India, when the nation is defined as a feminine form, as Bharat Mata, there is an emotional and cultural context to that definition. Nationalism, then, must be looked at with its etymological root *nasci* in mind. 'Nasci' means 'by birth'. And when a relationship as emotional as that of a mother and a child is being considered, all other concerns become subservient to these emotions.

Therefore, when, in one of the first public rallies together with the BJP, strong regionalist leaders like AGP's Prafulla Mahanta, AGP chief Atul Bora and BPF chief, Hagrama Mohilary, roared 'Bharat Mata ki jai', there was a victory already clinched. The numerical electoral victory was a by-product of this emotional win—the coming together of the Axomi Aai and Bharat Mata.

In that sense, the victory of the BJP in Assam represents an inflection point in the history of India.

How Will History Record the BJP's Surge in the North-east?

After the debacles in the Delhi and Bihar assembly elections, the on-ground cadre of the BJP had suffered a serious blow to its confidence and zeal. Not only did political opponents to the

BJP heightened this feeling of despondency with their attacks and jibes, the overall narrative of how the national party could stand no ground to the combined might of regional forces in politics, had made a serious dent in the political psyche of the party. In that respect, winning Assam, and more recently Manipur, went a long way in boosting the morale of the party karyakartas and volunteers.

However, the political victory in Assam was not just about an electoral win in a state but given the history of Assam politics, Assam victory marked a huge ideological win for the party. The effect of the victory was so huge that karyakartas and swayamsevaks working in lands as far away as Kerala were elated and enthusiastic about this feat. So, the victory of Assam for the BJP was not just about the record eighty-seven assembly seats it won but it was also about the joint roars of 'Jai Aai Axom' and 'Bharat Mata ki jai'.

The victory laid down lessons for social integration in other states where religious divides are sharp and stark. Local flavours, local leaders and local issues gained precedence and dominated the style of campaigning in Assam. It also successfully showcased that as a party, the BJP had a secret sauce to unite the local flavours of politics with national ideological goals. This proved that it is not always necessary to put Prime Minister Narendra Modi's neck on the frontline while campaigning for state-level elections. It also asserted that the sheen of an international leader of his stature should be used to dazzle the electoral scene and not to light up the entire campaign. However, the huge impact of Prime Minister Modi and his policies, the fandom his name and image invokes in the far-flung tribal belts and river islands went a long way in cementing the presence of the BJP as a truly pan-national party in India.

The Assam elections were crucial to seal BJP's acceptability in a non-traditional turf. It showcased that the face of the BJP was benign yet forceful, assertive yet without shrill voices and logical even in rhetoric. This election also meant the assertion of a change in the way in which elections are being managed and run in this country. History will see this election as a turning point for a new pan-national identity of the BJP.

The kind of an emphatic electoral victory that Assam clinched on 19 May 2016 has roots in a strong urge to succeed, to win. This urge can only be sustained by a perennial hunger that propels a continuous and consistent battle with a clear vision against all odds. In the case of Assam, cohesive nationalism was that one goal, for which generations of swayamsevaks and karyakartas sacrificed their lives, envisioning a victory as defining as this.

The Road Ahead

The massiveness of the Assam victory for the BJP also sent a very clear signal on two counts—that the politics in the coming days within India is going to be about Modi versus the rest and that it is possible for the BJP to take note of the threat and work on local alliances.

Despite the failure of the mahagathbandhan in Bihar, this is not a matter of political conjecture but common wisdom, that ever since Bihar, there has been an opportunistic attempt to turn the political atmosphere against the BJP. In Bihar, there was the giant juggernaut of the mahagathbandhan against the BJP, in Assam there was open talk about a maha-understanding against the BJP. In general, there has always been a united voice against the BJP across political spectrums on issues that affect electoral mandates.

This coalition of forces is not new to the Indian political scene. But it is a different kind of political coalition. Earlier, political coalitions were meant to form governments like the Atal Bihari Vajpayee–led coalition or the Manmohan Singh–led coalition. But this time, political coalition is meant to stop a government from being formed or to destabilize a democratically elected government.

It is true that a coalition of the mahagathbandhan type might again rear its head and pose an existential threat to the BJP, especially its electoral fortunes. But it is also true that an ideology-less alliance will have very little to offer in terms of longevity. Since the coalition is steeped in the politics of obstructionist political behaviour, it has little investment to offer to itself on common achievable goals. Herein lies a situation that the BJP must learn to exploit.

In Assam, for instance, as confessed by Maulana Badruddin Ajmal in a series of tweets,[2] an alliance between the AIUDF and the Congress did not happen despite Prashant Kishor's efforts to bring the two parties together. The BJP had pre-empted the move for a possible mahagathbandhan and had worked very closely with ears on ground to ensure that this time the BJP takes a lead. The result was a counter 'dream alliance'.

The work of the RSS, an ideological mentor to the BJP, for decades at a stretch without any affiliation to politics and electoral affinities in Assam, played a huge role in cementing this rainbow coalition for the BJP. Years of service among the people of various communities and tribes went a long way in ensuring a trust between the alliance partners as Shekhar Gupta pointed out.[3] The chemistry between the RSS and the BJP vis-à-vis Assam and the elections in 2016 showed a relationship that deserves to be a part of the political folklore, a blueprint of sorts, of how the BJP should expand itself.

Talking of coalitions, in a state like Jammu and Kashmir, the BJP and the Peoples Democratic Party are together with a common minimum government agenda despite huge ideological differences. Politically, these two states offer something else beyond just being poster faces of a BJP government in historically hostile terrains for the party. Political successes in these states demonstrate the creativity of the BJP's leadership in cultivating new common grounds that can accommodate divergent ideas.

The political learning from Assam most certainly is that it would work in favour of the BJP as it pre-empts the political situation in the coming days from its opposing camps. It would do the party a great service if the strategy decentralizes itself and focus is given to local alliances and dynamics than an attempt to dictate politics from the Centre.

New Electioneering

Ever since the effectiveness of how the 2014 general elections panned out in this country, there has been a growing trend of the youth getting involved in politics. And this involvement is more often than not, not electoral or in the realm of active politics. This involvement is more voluntary on grounds of part-time support or work for a political party, for which they passionately feel about. This has been recently documented by the Indian media as the involvement of young 'professionals' in politics. However, there is something that one needs to understand about this trend.

It is encouraging that in a country in which almost one-third of the population is young, where until now a mere 11 per cent of parliamentarians qualify as 'young', there has been a growing consciousness about politics and the imperative to participate in it. It is also interesting to see that while traditional roles of elected representatives remain coveted by the youth engaged in active politics, a sizeable number of youngsters have been coming out and doing their bit in impacting and asserting their voice in politics outside legislatures.

So, be it the India against Corruption movement, the mass uproar in the Nirbhaya case, the way in which young professionals campaigned during the general elections for the then prime ministerial candidate Narendra Modi, or today when many politically engaged satirical voices on social media impact public opinion, or even the way in which increasingly political parties are engaging youth and its services in politics, there has been considerable involvement of the youth in politics.

But another fact that needs to be confronted with this trend is the eulogizing of young 'professionals' in politics. Media, more often than not today, is hasty in driving at conclusions based on a few stories. Over the past two years, some sections, rather editors and senior journalists in our media, seem to have attributed far too much credence to poll strategists. Elections are a massive public exercise, which require Herculean efforts at various organizational levels. Undue credit to a few is an unprofessional assessment of several synergetic efforts required to win the elections.

As a young political professional largely disconnected from the real and hard world of electoral politics, one can do only a bit to impact political decisions on ground. It is unjust to take credit of the entire poll outcome of an election based on the professional prowess of a few data crunchers and advertising geniuses in boardrooms. It is unjust because the data on their dashboards are not magical entrants from ground on the basis of a few simulations. The blood and sweat of political workers who might not always have had the luxury of branded education and branded office spaces, but have transformed the stories of political change in poll booths over years of unnamed and unacknowledged work. To usurp that hard work within a few stories of accolades for oneself is dishonest.

It is unjust because there is nothing that has fundamentally changed about elections in India. Mass rallies have been successful even in the past without the Excel sheets showing a checklist with work in progress. Alliances and fallouts have happened between political parties in the past on paper and pen without a few external professional agencies analysing electoral trends on their laptops. To swallow the merits of old-fashioned and equally professional way of doing things in the glossy world of new technologies is unjust to generations of political workers who have been honest with their politics and their allegiance to their party for decades.

In no respect, one small, short-term team or pool of professionals should claim to be a kingmaker. Even before the concept of campaign managers came into play, political parties fought and won elections. They organized rallies, held big karyakarta meetings, managed hordes of volunteers. Are we saying they were not professional enough?

Every political worker brings with him a great set of experiences and ideas. In a party of more than 25,00,000 karyakartas in Assam, for instance, thousands of ideas were at play in full fruition, sometimes not even for any transactional benefit. Who would decide which one was professional and which one was not? Every bit of contribution added to the richness of this mandate-seeking exercise.

Data crunchers have the capability to offer prescriptions based on numbers. But what about chemistry which works to translate prescriptions into suggestive reality? A silent but sustained sociopolitical and socio-economic revolution has been simmering on in Assam over decades through Ekal Vidyalays, Lok Jagaran Manch and so many other organizations. Millions of swayamsevaks have sacrificed their lives at the altar of selfless service in tribal areas of the state to see this day. Can professional data crunchers' one time dashboard substitute these sacrifices?

Having said this, it is true that young professional volunteers add dynamism and a sense of urgency to an election process. It is also true that this cadre of workers on a sabbatical from their regular jobs, who do not treat politics as a fulltime vocation but come together to impact electoral outcomes decisively, add a selfless and innovative dimension to the process of electioneering.

With no direct stake in constituencies, they often bounce off politically bold and innovative ideas beyond the ideation realm of traditionalists within the party. They are fearless of failing and courageous to commit mistakes and most certainly are really passionate about what they propose to do. More often than not, the one election where they come to volunteer their services becomes a personal battle for them—something that traditional party karyakartas miss out on in the inevitable case that every election is one among many that they have to fight.

It is also true that this new age, technology-savvy and politically engaged volunteer who comes with a shelf life for that election cycle, is able to articulate ideas which are incisive, focused and implementable at scale. The corporate-world experiences that these volunteers bring in help launch and execute small innovative projects at scale, which go a long way in contributing to the overall efforts by the party.

There is a demand for mentorship across the board in every field, most specifically politics. The stalwarts in the field of politics or the innovative minds within the political space or those politicians who look beyond their own generation to invest in the future of this nation, must come forward to nurture young and interested professionals in politics. With the world order in India increasingly organizing itself amidst the chaotic cacophony of dissenting and competing voices, it is important that political parties allow youngsters to learn and contribute beyond the traditional world of morchas, *prakoshth*s (cells) and wings. A possible leaf could be taken from American politics where different political parties invest in nurturing caucuses and encourage volunteering and/or short-term internships, especially during elections.

Voters versus Consumers

Having discussed at length the interaction between volunteerism and politics, it is crucial to point out that anyone working in this space should have the humility to respect the emotions with which people come out and vote. This goes for those people as well who serve like part-time volunteers or as professional campaign managers loaned out to a party for a specific period of time or those people who contribute to the process with an ideology-free mindset of issue-based politics.

As responsible and aware citizens, the real impact that we could make in politics would be to impact elections and politics qualitatively than just quantitatively. The youth could impact politics in a meaningful way only if elections move out from being a game of numbers played out every five years to being an exercise in accountability and reflection. The youth could impact electoral outcomes with responsible participation only if the erstwhile notion of looking at people as vote banks is replaced by the real concern of people and their thoughts, something that Sanjay Paswan calls 'thought banks'.

Of late, electoral strategies have focused on treating voters as consumers. Like an advertising project, every election is meant to focus on a cross-section of vote banks where youth, women, religious communities et al. are treated as separate segments. Freebies, dole-outs and rhetoric help run focused ad campaigns to capture the mind space of these voters and psychologically impact voting-day outcomes.

It is unfortunate that in the process of these packaged formulae at play, an individual citizen is stripped of his/her identity at an intersection of these target groups. For instance, a woman is rarely a youth, a Dalit, a Muslim, a Hindu, a tribal, an entrepreneur, a government job aspirant, etc. She is always a woman first for whom a certain manifesto point to be coined. Similarly, it goes for all the separate, dominant target groups a campaigner thinks of while designing the marketing plan.

It is unfortunate and dangerous for democracy. With these sharp and incisive tools at the disposal of the campaigners, the effort should be to look at holistic politics with issues of governance and development at the helm. However, the focus so far has most certainly been on winning over chunks from here and there so as to stitch a pastiche of winnable constituencies.

We must remember that voters are not consumers. The battle for ideologies is bigger than what market dynamics can ever fathom. Marketing tools and the knowledge to utilize those tools pump in efficiency into the system, but the DNA of the system is embedded in the ideological commitment to universal ideals.

The Global Battles of Saraighat

The issue of migration, which occupied the centre stage of political discourse in 2016 surpassed the boundaries of national concerns. It reflected upon a global phenomenon of political conversations that discuss the issue of migration beyond the economics of it. It opened up the discussion a little more around the cultural aspects of a society, about pride in, and genuine efforts towards cultural resurgence.

In several Western countries like Germany, the USA, Australia, France and the UK, migration has moved out of the globalization tinder box to initiate a conversation on the politics of migration. The argument of a global village with melting-pot societies celebrating multiculturalism is being increasingly challenged by electoral mandates. The idea of political correctness, which prevents one from talking about concerns that afflict the masses, which casts risks on being open and transparent about feelings and situations, is increasingly going for a toss. Civilizational uniqueness has been erased in the liberal narrative of tolerance, which is good in its own right, but has come with a set of unaddressed identity questions. The possible problems which the processes and advocates of globalization pushed under the rug then have begun to surface now—decades later.

While the West has been grappling with the altered demographic profile due to the recent spate of political migration by less than 1 per cent, one can imagine the scale of push back from within the community, in Assam, in a situation where one-third of the population has become that of migrants. Relegated to the margins in the political and policy imagination of the successive ruling dispensations, the indigenous people of Assam face a grave threat to their identity and a more pronounced problem of competing with outsiders over asserting economic and political standpoints.

Unfortunately, no structured study has been undertaken by any think tank dedicated to studying this concern over time in India. Academic papers, government reports and journalistic exercises expatiating on the issue of migration in Assam have been either heavily lopsided with ideological moorings and/or invested in a time constrained completion of the project.

The migrant situation in Germany, the staggering figure of 80 per cent asylum seekers having no documents, comes as a shock. Further, articles on demographic profiling and the cultural crisis in Germany were telling of the latent and vexed issues with respect to migration, assimilation and integration.

Brexit informed the world at large about the hypocrisies of the liberal claim of civilizations being tolerant and being a melting pot of cultures. The hatred and passionate emotions with which Britain voted suggests a perceptible shift in the political discourse with respect to the situation of migrants across Europe.

Even in the USA, the issue of migration became the sole emotional concern to decide on its presidential elections. The issue of assimilation and integration of migrants with the local population was deeply contested across concepts of cultural hegemony and felt realities of economic ramifications.

The mainstreaming of the issue of migration around the regular political narrative is symptomatic of a larger problem that world is grappling with. Beyond the rhetoric of an electoral mandate, there has to be political pre-emption in discussing the issue at hand. We need to have a free and non-judgemental deliberation on the issue that will require shifting the linguistic and ideological boundaries beyond what we have grown to appreciate and critique within.

The Assam elections showcased that the election was not just about the Battle of Saraighat fought on the banks of the Brahmaputra but about similar battles being fought on the banks of the Hudson and the Thames, among others.

NOTES

~

INTRODUCTION

1. Conversations with Dr Nani Gopal Mahanta, head of department, political science, Gauhati University, Guwahati, Assam.

CHAPTER 1: A HISTORY OF POLITICAL BLUNDERS

1. Sandipan Sharma, 'Assam Assembly Polls 2016: Amit Shah and the art of sacrificing facts at the altar of election campaigning', Firstpost.com, 18 May 2016, http://bit.ly/2wB3nlo.
2. Udayon Misra, *The Periphery Strikes Back: Challenges to the Nation-State in Assam and Nagaland* (Shimla: Indian Institute of Advanced Study, 2000), 86.
3. The Assam Association, formed in 1903, served as the mouthpiece of the Assamese middle class in articulating their needs and aspirations.
4. Mahanta quoting Kedarnath Goswami, 'Assam's Rubber Stamp Leadership', the *Assam Tribune*, 8 January 1948, 14.
5. Nani Gopal Mahanta, *Confronting the State: Ulfa's Quest for Sovereignty* (New Delhi: SAGE Publications, 2013), 6.
6. Misra, *The Periphery Strikes Back*, 80.

7. Sunil Pawan Baruah, 'Role of the Press in the Nationalist Upsurge—Brahmaputra Valley', in *Nationalist Upsurge in Assam*, eBook, ed. Arun Bhuyan (Guwahati: Government of Assam, August 2000), 330–31.

8. File No. p 4 (i)—1937, AICC Files, Nehru Memorial Museum and Library, referred to in Girin Phukan, *Politics of Regionalism in Northeast India* (Guwahati: Spectrum, 1996), 73.

9. 'National anthem needs scrutiny: Deka', the *Assam Tribune*, 17 September 2011, http://bit.ly/2f5BMCE.

10. Nirode K. Barooah, *Gopinath Bordoloi: 'The Assam Problem' and Nehru's Centre* (Assam: Bhabani Books, 2010), 52.

11. Bordoloi's private diary, dated 17 March 1941, as quoted by Mahadev Sarma, op. cit., 90–95: 'I am astonished to know that even C. Reddy, the vice chancellor of the University of Andhra Pradesh thinks that Assam is a Muslim-majority state.'

12. Dr Nirode K. Barooah, *Gopinath Bardoloi: Indian Constitution and Centre–Assam relations, 1940–1945* (Assam: Publication Board of Assam, 1989), 25.

13. Ibid.

14. Id.

15. Id., 27.

16. Id.

17. Assam Provincial Congress Committee Papers, 1946; *Political History of Assam*, vol. III, 380.

18. Mahanta, *Confronting the State*, 20.

19. 'Transfer of Power: IX, 510', quoted by Mahanta in *Confronting the State*, 20.

20. 'Star of India', 4 May 1946, cited in *Political History of Assam*, vol. III, 279.

21. S.L. Baruah, *A Comprehensive History of Assam* (New Delhi: Munshiram Manoharlal Publishers, 1995), 612.

22. Amit Shah at a public meeting in Lakhimpur, Assam, 28 March 2016.

23. Gopinath Bordoloi in his interview with the Cabinet Mission and Viceroy Wavell on 1 April 1946; see Bordoloi Papers.

24. Baruah, *A Comprehensive History of Assam*, 598.

25. Ibid.

26. Ved Prakash, *Terrorism in India's Northeast: A Gathering Storm* (New Delhi: Kalpaz Publications, 2008), 318.

27. Nirode K. Barooah, *Gopinath Bardoloi, 'The Assam Problem' and Nehru's Centre* (Guwahati: Bhabani Books, 2010), 53.

28. Barooah, *Gopinath Bardoloi*, 30.

29. Barooah, *Gopinath Bordoloi*, Nehru to Bordoloi letters, New Delhi, dated 18 May 1949, 30.

30. Ibid.

31. Barooah, *Gopinath Bordoloi*, Bordoloi to Nehru (Secret Letter), Shillong, 24 August 1949, 33–34.

32. Barooah, *Gopinath Bordoloi*, 34.

33. Mahanta, *Confronting the State*, 46.

34. Bitasta Das, 'ULFA's Xhunor Axom and Negation of the State', *Artha: Journal of Social Sciences* 13, no. 3 (2014): 31–42.

35. Barooah, *Gopinath Bordoloi*, 29.

CHAPTER 2: THE RUN-UP TO THE 2016 ELECTIONS

1. Praveen Patil, 'The North-Eastern Sunrise of Hindu Polity', 5forty3.in, 3 April 2016, http://bit.ly/2y9eCT9.

2. Sanjib Barua, *India against Itself: Assam and the Politics of Nationality (Critical Histories)* (Pennsylvania: University of Pennsylvania Press, 1999), 118.

3. Amalendu Guha, *Planter Raj to Swaraj: Freedom Struggle and Electoral Politics in Assam 1826–1947* (New Delhi: Indian Council of Historical Research, 1977), 206.

4. Barua, *India against Itself*, 128.

5. *See* Barua, *India against Itself*, 129: 'The Taimur government tried to discipline ethnic Assamese government employees, especially senior officials who were known sympathizers of the movement . . .

In order to use more force against the movement, Taimur effectively had to transform the state bureaucracy. For instance, her personal secretariat, it was reported, had only Muslim professionals. These measures accentuated the legitimacy crisis in the state.'

6. Barua, *India against Itself*, 114.
7. Barua, *India against Itself*, 127.
8. Barua, *India against Itself*, 126.
9. Arun Shourie, 'Assam Elections: Come What May', *India Today*, 15 May 1983, http://bit.ly/2wsTL0U.
10. Barua, *India against Itself*, quoting the lyrics of Bhupen Hazarika's Assamese song, 149.
11. Paresh Barua in an interview with BBC correspondent Subir Bhaumik, *The Week*, referred to in *Swadhinota* by Parag Moni Aditya, 35, and referred to in Mahanta, *Confronting the State*, 87.
12. Barua, *India against Itself*, 135.
13. Pravin Patil, 'United Spectrum of Hindu Assam!', 5forty3.in, 11 April 2016, http://bit.ly/2wBscgU.
14. Nani Gopal Mahanta, *Confronting the State: ULFA's Quest for Sovereignty* (New Delhi: SAGE Publications, 2013), 98.
15. Ibid., 99.
16. 'Blames Mahanta for "secret killings" in Assam', *The Hindu*, 12 March 2016, http://bit.ly/2fewkki.
17. Samudra Gupta Kashyap, 'Assam's "secret killings": Tarun Gogoi plays 15-yr-old hand again', the *Indian Express*, 1 April 2016, http://bit.ly/2ylijX1.
18. Kaushik Deka, 'Perfume baron Ajmal sniffs out votes in "secret pact with Assam Chief Minister"', Mail Online India, 7 April 2014, http://dailym.ai/2hd4thr.
19. Interview with Himanta Biswa Sarma, 29 November 2016, Goa.
20. Abhishek Chakraborty, 'Rahul Gandhi Likes Servant–Master Relationship, says Himanta Biswa Sarma', NDTV.com, 19 May 2016, http://bit.ly/2hahuvV.
21. Interview with Himanta Biswa Sarma, 29 November 2016, Goa.
22. Ibid.

CHAPTER 3: FIVE DECADES OF THE SANGH

1. Ravish Kumar's show, *Prime Time*, on NDTV, 19 May 2016, http://bit.ly/2y9mwMk.
2. Kshetriya pracharak is a notch higher than the prant pracharak. The former oversees the activities of a couple of regions.
3. Based on interviews with senior RSS workers.
4. 'ULFAr Sabhapotir Boktvya', statement by the ULFA chairman released on 8 May 1990.
5. Ajit Kumar Bhuyan, 'Flames of Freedom Still Burning: A Probe into the National Question in India', in *Symphony of Freedom: Papers on Nationality Question*, All India People's Resistance Forum (AIPRF), presented at the International Seminar, 16–19 February 1996, New Delhi, 56.
6. Parag Kumar Das, *Rastradruhir Dinlipi*, 26.
7. Udayon Misra, *The Periphery Strikes Back: Challenges to the Nation-State in Assam and Nagaland* (Shimla: Indian Institute of Advanced Study, 2000), 78.
8. Nani Gopal Mahanta, *Confronting the State: ULFA's Quest for Sovereignty* (New Delhi: SAGE Publications, 2013), 139.
9. With inputs from RSS prant pracharak, Assam, Baisistha Bujarbaruah.
10. Malini Bhattacharya, 'Tracing the Emergence and Consolidation of Hindutva in Assam', *Economic & Political Weekly*, 16 April 2016, http://bit.ly/2fux8hY.

CHAPTER 4: GETTING BATTLE-READY

1. Sangeeta Barooah Pisharoty, 'High Stakes for BJP and Congress in the Fragrant Tea Gardens of Upper Assam', the *Wire*, 3 April 2016, http://bit.ly/2wBCTjF.
2. Ibid.
3. Jayeeta Sharma, *Empire's Garden: Assam and the Making of India (Radical Perspectives)* (Durham, NC: Duke University Press, 2011), 235.

4. 'Exemptions to minority community nationals from Bangladesh and Pakistan in regularization of their entry and stay in India', Press Information Bureau, 7 September 2015, http://bit.ly/2f61Qxr.

5. '"Outsider" Mahendra Singh who changed Assam's Political Equation', the *Economic Times*, 26 May 2016, http://bit.ly/2y9PYSy.

6. Ibid.

7. Swagata Sen and Arun Shourie, 'May 15, 1983: Come what may', *India Today*, 18 December 2006, http://bit.ly/2w3gcVT.

8. Rahul Karmakar, 'Congress not sole claimant of Ali-Kuli-Bongali vote bank in Assam', the *Hindustan Times*, 4 April 2016, http://bit.ly/2gdqbWn.

9. Pisharoty, 'High Stakes for BJP and Congress', the *Wire*.

10. Manoj Anand, 'Ahead of polls, BJP conducts its 1st Assam Nirman meet', *Asian Age*, 30 January 2016, http://bit.ly/2yjUO0p.

11. C&AG Report on State Finances—Assam, 2015.

12. Samudra Gupta Kashyap, 'Assam polls will be showdown "between Modi and me", says Tarun Gogoi', the *Indian Express*, 9 February 2016, http://bit.ly/1Q3jwlI.

13. 2011 Census Data, Census of India, http://bit.ly/2f62riF.

14. BJP Assam Pradesh (@BJP4Assam), Twitter post, 17 January 2016, 6.16 a.m., http://bit.ly/2xLsO8J: '@tarun_gogoi rule: 96% agricultural land in Assam has no irrigation facilities #15YearsOfLoot #15YearsOfDestruction'.

15. Debendra Upadhyay, Twitter post, 13 January 2016, 8.57 a.m., http://bit.ly/2haRwZ5: '@TheHindu Bogibeel bridge over Brahmaputra is an utter negligence of congress govt in Assam. #15yearsofloot'.

16. Sarat Sarma, 'Cong–BJP in hoarding war', the *Telegraph*, 3 March 2016, http://bit.ly/2wCyVr1.

17. An anecdote that came up from discussions we had with a taxi driver in Guwahati on 20 February 2016.

18. Prabin Kalita, 'Congress uses face of Gujarat riots in Assam campaign', the *Times of India*, 10 April 2016, http://bit.ly/2xao3EW.

19. Ibid.

20. '"Face" of Gujarat riots Qutubuddin Ansari miffed with political parties, says "stop using me"', Zee News India, 12 April 2016, http://bit.ly/2f67qzH.

CHAPTER 5: BATTLING THE WAR

1. Samudra Gupta Kashyap, 'Assam: Intellectuals appeal to vote against BJP kicks up row', the *Indian Express*, 3 April 2016, http://bit.ly/2ylpspZ. The petition of the intellectuals was referred to as a 'fatwa' by other leading group of intellectuals, which included former Gauhati University vice chancellor Nirmal Kumar Choudhury and former Assam DGP Nishinath Changkakoti.

2. 'Will leave India if Modi becomes PM: Kannada writer Ananthamurthy', *Indian Express*, 19 September 2013, http://bit.ly/2f6PoNW.

3. 'Ananthamurthy awaiting Congress's response to his offer', *The Hindu*, 16 March 2004, http://bit.ly/2xuhg95.

4. Pravin Patil, 'United Spectrum of Hindu Assam!', 5forty3.in, 11 April 2016, http://bit.ly/2wBscgU.

5. Umanand Jaiswal, 'Self-styled kingmaker Ajmal loses, blow to AIUDF', the *Telegraph*, 20 May 2016, http://bit.ly/2ylZcf5

6. Naresh Mitral, 'Stunned Ajmal grapples with loss', the *Times of India*, 21 May 2016, http://bit.ly/2ffzyV0.

7. Jaiswal, 'Self-styled kingmaker Ajmal loses', the *Telegraph*.

8. Saurav Bora and Avishek Sengupta, 'Cong heartbreak in bastions: 4-fold cheer for BJP in capital', the *Telegraph*, 19 May 2016, http://bit.ly/2yajebS.

9. Rajiv Konwar, 'AGP emerges from 15-year *bonobax*', the *Telegraph*, 19 May 2016, http://bit.ly/2xdlT5l.

10. Preetam B. Choudhury, 'BPF sweeps all 12 seats in Bodo belt', the *Telegraph*, 19 May 2016, http://bit.ly/2f6wruC.

11. Pullock Dutta, 'Alliance gamble that paid off: Bridge hope rests on Sonowal', the *Telegraph*, 19 May 2016, http://bit.ly/2w4BAdJ.

12. V. Kumara Swamy, Sonia Sarkar and Prasun Chaudhuri, 'Sowing saffron, reaping lotus', the *Telegraph*, 22 May 2016, http://bit.ly/2ffAyIK.

13. Shekhar Gupta, 'Assam's 35-year saffronisation', *Business Standard*, 9 April 2016, http://bit.ly/1TGpSxV.

CHAPTER 6: ELECTIONS AND INDIAN DEMOCRACY

1. Pravin Patil, 'United Spectrum of Hindu Assam!', 5forty3.in, 11 April 2016, http://bit.ly/2wBscgU.

2. 'Badruddin Ajmal holds Congress responsible if BJP wins in Assam', the *Economic Times*, 12 April 2016, http://bit.ly/2wrWSpE.

3. Shekhar Gupta, 'Assam's 35-year saffronisation', *Business Standard*, 9 April 2016, http://bit.ly/1TGpSxV.